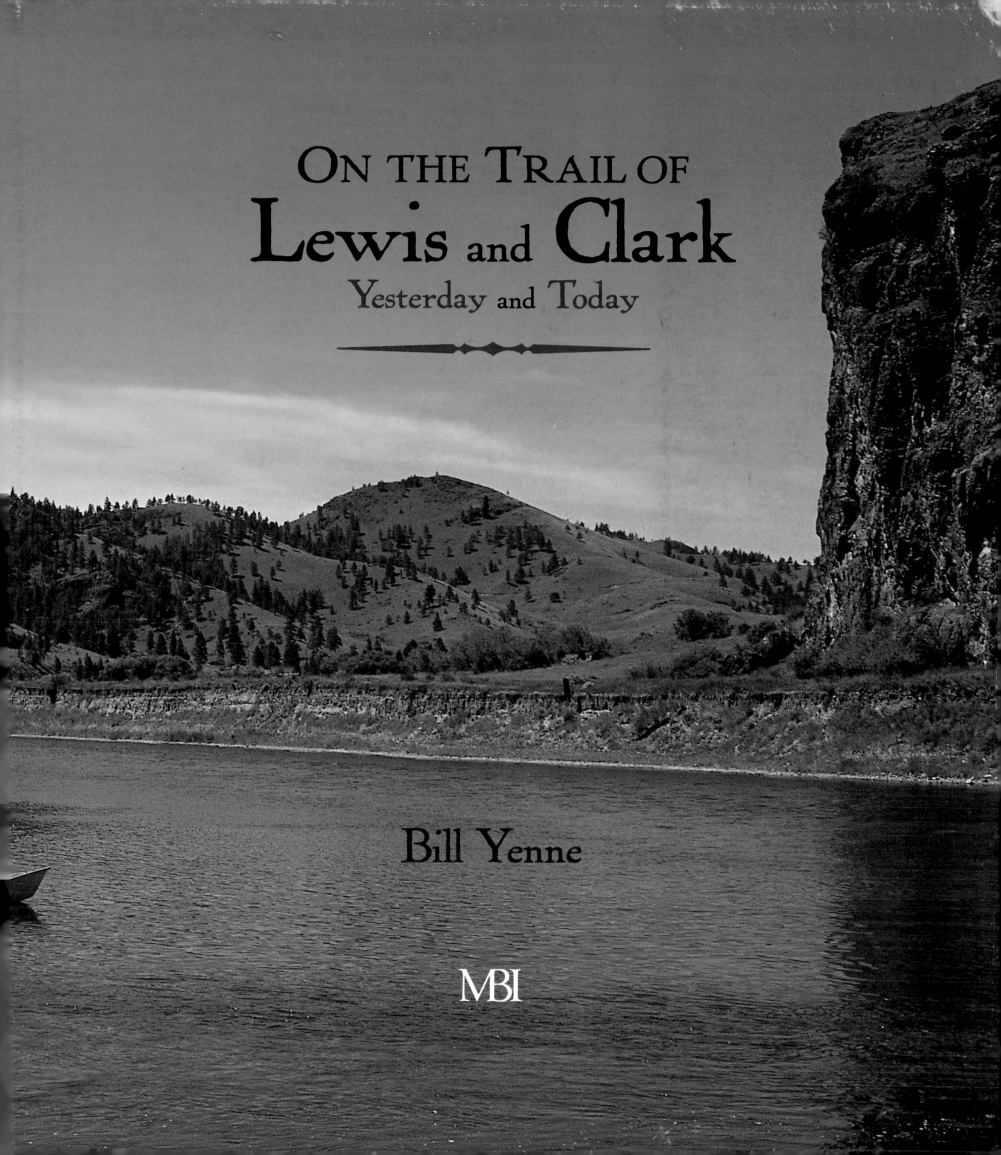

ON THE TRAIL OF
Lewis and Clark
Yesterday and Today

Bill Yenne

MBI

First published in 2005 by MBI, an imprint of MBI
Publishing Company, Galtier Plaza, Suite 200, 380
Jackson Street, St. Paul, MN 55101-3885 USA

MBI titles are also available at discounts in bulk quantity
for industrial or sales-promotional use. For details write
to Special Sales Manager at MBI Publishing Company
Wholesalers & Distributors, Galtier Plaza, Suite 200, 380
Jackson Street, St. Paul, MN 55101-3885 USA.

ISBN 0-7603-2002-0

Editorial: Dennis Pernu and Amy Glaser
Design: Mandy Iverson and Tom Heffron

Printed in China

On the frontispiece: Silhouetted against a Prairie sunset,
a Lewis and Clark expedition re-enactor gestures toward
a distant western horizon. *Chad Coppess, South Dakota
Department of Tourism*

On the title page: A timeless view of a boater resting on
an island in the upper Missouri River upstream from
Great Falls, Montana. Lewis and Clark passed this place
in their dugout canoes during the third week of July 1805.
Bill Yenne

On the back cover

Bottom middle: Named for Clark's nickname for
Sacagawea's baby, Pompey's Pillar is the highest overlook
along the Yellowstone River for many miles in the section
of the river between present-day Billings and Miles City.
It was an important site for the Crow people, who
referred to it as the place "Where the Mountain Lion
Preys." *Bill Yenne*

Bottom right: In the State of Idaho, the signs that mark
U.S. Highway 12 (aka the Lewis and Clark Highway) are
color-coded in brown to identify the road as a historic
highway. *Bill Yenne*

Top left: This 12-foot bronze statue of Sacagawea and her
son, Jean Baptiste, was created by Chicago artist Leonard
Crunelle and was dedicated on October 13, 1910. Located
on the grounds of the North Dakota state capitol in
Bismarck, it depicts a woman somewhat older than
Sacagawea was when she traveled west with Lewis and
Clark. She is generally believed to have been about 16 in
1804. *Bill Yenne*

Contents

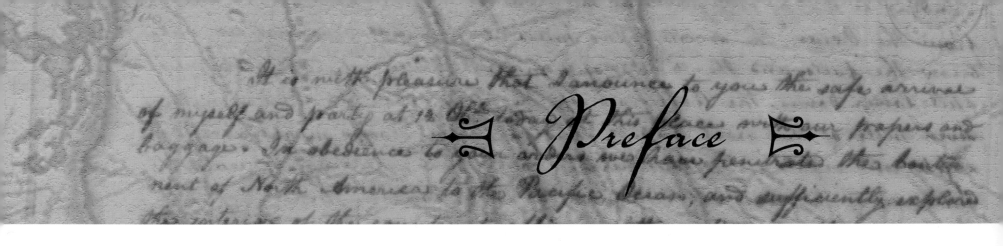

The author (right) and his friend Bill Dakin are on a bluff overlooking the northernmost point reached by either Meriwether Lewis or William Clark on their epic expedition. Lewis called this place on Cut Bank Creek Cape Disappointment because the creek did not continue north into Canada. Because of the overcast weather, Lewis and his party camped here four nights and waited for the clouds to part so they could take a sextant reading. The Rocky Mountains within Montana's Glacier National Park are barely visible in the distance.

Author collection

"It's a good thing that Jefferson didn't send us."

That phrase was spoken in desperation as we bounced down a gravel road that crossed the windswept plains of northern Montana, about 20 miles south of the Alberta line and 150 miles from civilization.

The object of our exercise that day was to find Camp Disappointment, the place on Cut Bank Creek that marked the northernmost point reached by Lewis and Clark and the Corps of Discovery. Actually, it was just Meriwether Lewis, along with George Drouillard and Joseph and Reubin Field, who camped here on July 22, 1806. The captains had split up on July 3, and William Clark was several hundred miles south, making his way east toward the mouth of the Yellowstone River at that time.

The object of Lewis' exercise two centuries before us had been to discover if the watershed of the Missouri River—acquired by Thomas Jefferson as part of the Louisiana Purchase—reached north, above 50 degrees north latitude, into the rich beaver-trapping region that is now Alberta. It was here on Cut Bank Creek that Lewis was disappointed to find that the Louisiana Purchase did not reach north of 50 degrees.

Now, here I was, traveling with my old friend, Bill Dakin, in the footsteps of Lewis, and we couldn't seem to find our way to the site of Lewis' Camp Disappointment!

"It's a good thing that Jefferson didn't send us," Bill said, implying that if Jefferson had sent us, rather than Lewis and Clark, then the greatest expedition in American history would not have gone as well as it had.

Our exploits that day would include numerous adventures that went beyond merely being lost on a gravel road. They would range from being at the mercy of a kindly Blackfeet woman, to being hopelessly stuck in 18 inches of mud. Thanks to the help of our newfound friend and our own ingenuity, we escaped the clutches of the mud and reached our goal.

We were not disappointed. Ultimately, we did find Camp Disappointment that day, and along with it, a sense of kinship with our predecessors two centuries before. Nearly two hours after abandoning the warm cocoon of our late-model Buick to travel overland, we stood amid the bones of cattle—who had died in the winter's snowdrifts—on the same site where Lewis had camped for three days two centuries before. Thanks to his careful calculations and meticulous notes, we knew that we were in the right place. Even Thomas Jefferson might have been proud of his twenty-first-century countrymen.

It was at that moment, as I stood upon that place, that I was bitten by the bug to travel the entire route of the Corps of Discovery. I decided at that moment that I would do the whole itinerary—from Camp Dubois, on the Mississippi near St. Louis, where it all began, to Fort Clatsop, where the Columbia River empties into the Pacific Ocean.

Acknowledgments

I thank the many people and organizations who were vital in supplying information, assistance, and material during the course of this work. Specifically, I thank the following people: David Borlaug, president of the Lewis and Clark Fort Mandan Foundation; Steve Boody of Boody Fine Arts in St. Louis, Missouri; Jennifer Bottomly-O'Looney of the Montana Historical Society; Chad Coppess of South Dakota Tourism and State Development; Robert Cox of the American Philosophical Society; Shane Culpepper of the Gilcrease Museum; Jill Harding at the Fort Clatsop National Monument; Pat Kennedy; Becka Kohl of the Montana Historical Society; Andrea Ashby Leraris of Independence National Historical Park; Paul Lloyd-Davies of the Lewis and Clark National Historic Trail Center in Great Falls, Montana; Wade V. Myers of the National Park Service, Harpers Ferry Center; Deputy Bob Perry of the McKenzie County (North Dakota) Sheriff's Office; Patricia A. Philips of the U.S. Geological Survey in Reston, Virginia; Marcia Poole of the Sioux City (South Dakota) Lewis and Clark Interpretive Center; Donnie Sexton of Travel Montana; Karen D. Stevens of Independence NHP; Callie Morfeld Vincent of the Amon Carter Museum in Fort Worth, Texas; Francis Weigand at Traveler's Rest State Park, Montana; and Brad Winn of the Lewis and Clark State Historic Site in Hartford, Illinois.

This photo was taken near Cape Disappointment at the end of the Lewis and Clark trail in Pacific County, Washington. *Bill Yenne*

Notes on Mileposts

The mileposts that we give throughout this text are based on the odometer readings recorded by the author when he made the drive from Camp Dubois in Illinois to the mouth of the Columbia River in June and July 2004. These are clearly an approximation of the actual route distances and are provided as a reference of relative distances. In the course of driving the Lewis and Clark Trail, the path follows rivers that have changed course many times in the past two centuries and travels on roads that cannot and do not follow the rivers precisely.

There are often several choices of roads to use to follow the rivers, and for several hundred miles in Montana, no roads follow the Missouri River at all. The Lewis and Clark Trail, as officially marked to varying degrees by the 11 states through which it runs, has no mileposts, and the signs marking the route frequently appear on two or more parallel roads.

Even our Milepost 1 at Camp Dubois is an approximation. The exact location of the original campsite is not known and is now probably under the Mississippi River. However, the replica of Camp Dubois, which marks our Milepost 1, is probably within a few miles of the original.

It is entirely possible, indeed probable, that someone driving the route will have differing odometer readings. We hope that this book will inspire all of our readers to start out from—or near—Camp Dubois and let their odometers roll all the way to the mouth of the Columbia River.

The Lewis and Clark trail along U.S. Highway 87 in Cascade County, Montana. *Bill Yenne*

Notes on Spelling

The quotes from the writings of Lewis and Clark that are included in this work generally retain the original spellings that they used. The Lewis and Clark Expedition occurred in an era before the formal adoption of standardized spelling, and the captains did most of their writing in conditions where most of us would not always use correct spelling. They spelled the same word many different ways and used numerous abbreviations. Retaining the misspelling and bad grammar is customary when quoting the captains, although it is unfair. Mostly, the journals were written in the field, literally, and often in adverse conditions or by the light of a flickering candle. Had the captains been sitting in a comfortable drawing room, or at a modern word processor, they probably would have done a better job. But consistent spelling was not in the job description, the content was. The content of their journals is, considering the circumstances under which it was compiled, one of the most important documentary efforts in history.

The Lewis and Clark trail west of Lolo Pass in Idaho County, Idaho. *Bill Yenne*

... the expences of transportation over this portage to a mere trifle.

... the navigation of the Roschasshe, the South East branch of the ...

Introduction

This is the story of the trail taken by men who naively believed that the tools and science of the eighteenth-century enlightenment could be used to conquer unlimited time and space in places where nobody from their civilization had gone before.

It is the story of men who heroically persisted, even when they realized the huge magnitude of their underestimation of time and space. This is the story of the time and space when they ultimately succeeded in their goal two centuries ago.

In the words of Meriwether Lewis, this place is the "essential point in the geography of this western part of the Continent." The primary goal assigned to Lewis by President Thomas Jefferson was to explore the extent of the Missouri River and reach this point, the place where it begins. An epic 14 months after they left the mouth of the Missouri, Lewis and Clark stood here at its headwaters. At this spot near Three Forks, Montana, the Jefferson, Madison, and Gallatin rivers flow together to form the Missouri. *Bill Yenne*

The Lewis and Clark trail near Washburn in McLean County, North Dakota. *Bill Yenne*

The 1804–1806 expedition, undertaken by the Corps of Discovery and led by Captain Meriwether Lewis and Captain William Clark, is one of the truly monumental epics from the formative years of the United States. No discussion of the history of the American West is complete without mention of it in the opening pages.

Lewis and Clark redefined American geography and the American sense of identity. They were probably the first human beings to travel the entire breadth of what is now the United States, and they penetrated for more than a thousand miles into territory that was unknown to anyone who resided within the 17 states that comprised the United States at that time.

The two captains and their men spent 28 months in the field, covered more than 8,000 miles, and accomplished the goals set out for their expedition by President Thomas Jefferson. Primarily, these goals were to locate the headwaters of the Missouri River and explore the region between these headwaters and the Pacific Ocean. Not only did Lewis and Clark accomplish these goals, but they returned with the bonus of an immense store of scientific data about this vast region that was heretofore unknown. They surveyed uncharted mountain ranges, explored rivers that had never appeared on maps, and reported the details of numerous plant and animal species that were "new to science."

Equally amazing was that they endured two difficult winters, overcame incredible physical obstacles and hardships, and returned to their starting point having lost just a single member of their expedition. That man died of appendicitis, which would have probably been fatal even if he had been in Philadelphia or Washington when it occurred.

The amazing success of the Lewis and Clark project is attributable to the skilled leadership of the two captains and to the tenacity and unity of the group of men who made the full 28-month round trip. It is also attributable to incredible good luck, and in no small measure, to a remarkable and enigmatic Shoshone teenager known as Sacagawea.

Stories of trails are the cornerstones of the mythology of American westward expansion, and the Lewis and Clark Trail is the cornerstone upon which all of the subsequent Western trails were built. In the early days of American expansion, the trails were just as likely to be on water as on land, such is the case with the Lewis and Clark Expedition. Their mandate was their trail. It began and ended with the Missouri River and included the Columbia River. The vast Missouri River system drains one sixth of the United States and, according to the U.S. Geological Survey, flows 2,341 miles from its headwaters at the confluence of the Gallatin, Madison, and Jefferson rivers at Three Forks, Montana, to its confluence with the Mississippi River at St. Louis.

This rugged hillside is in the Bitterroot Range, where Lewis and Clark trekked through waist-deep snow in September 1805. *Bill Yenne*

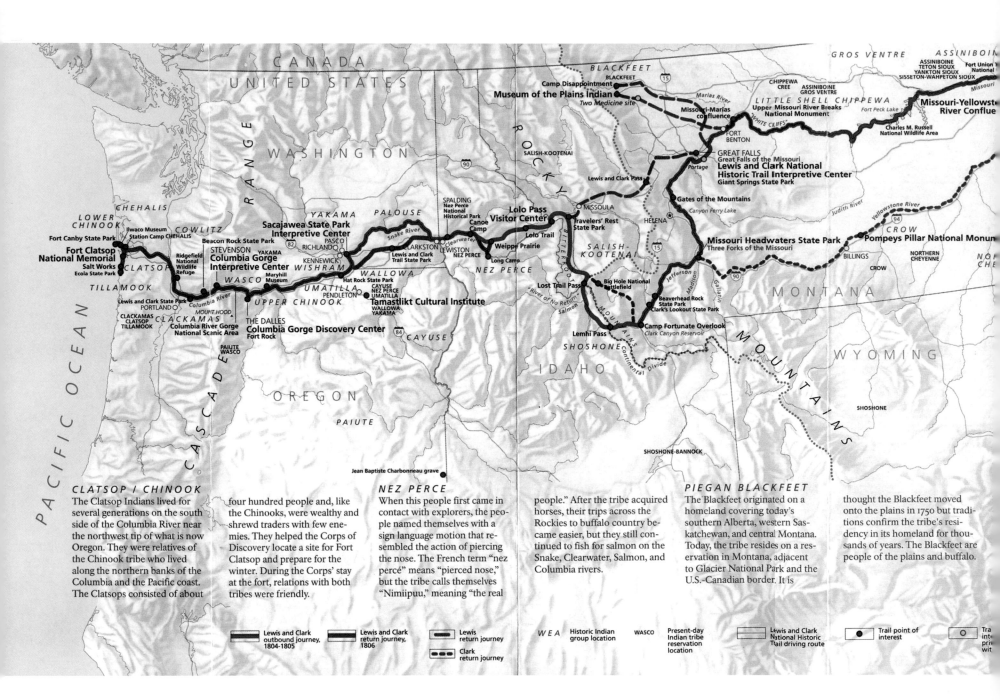

This is the official National Park Service map of the Lewis and Clark Trail that shows contemporary sites related to the expedition. *National Park Service, courtesy of Wade V. Myers, Harpers Ferry Center*

The Columbia, though half as long, makes up for this in volume. The U.S. Geological Survey Circular 1246 has some interesting statistics on the subject. In the days of Lewis and Clark, and up to the dam-building that changed both rivers in the mid-twentieth century, the peak volume of the Columbia at the Dalles was about 600,000 cubic feet per second. Meanwhile, the peak volume of the Missouri at Omaha, where it is fed by the Platte River, was 70,000 cubic feet per second. Today, the volume of the dammed Columbia is still more than quadruple that of the dammed Missouri.

Traveling the Lewis and Clark route today is like stepping back in time. The 11-state route conjures up an era before cellular telephones. Indeed, much of this area is so remote that

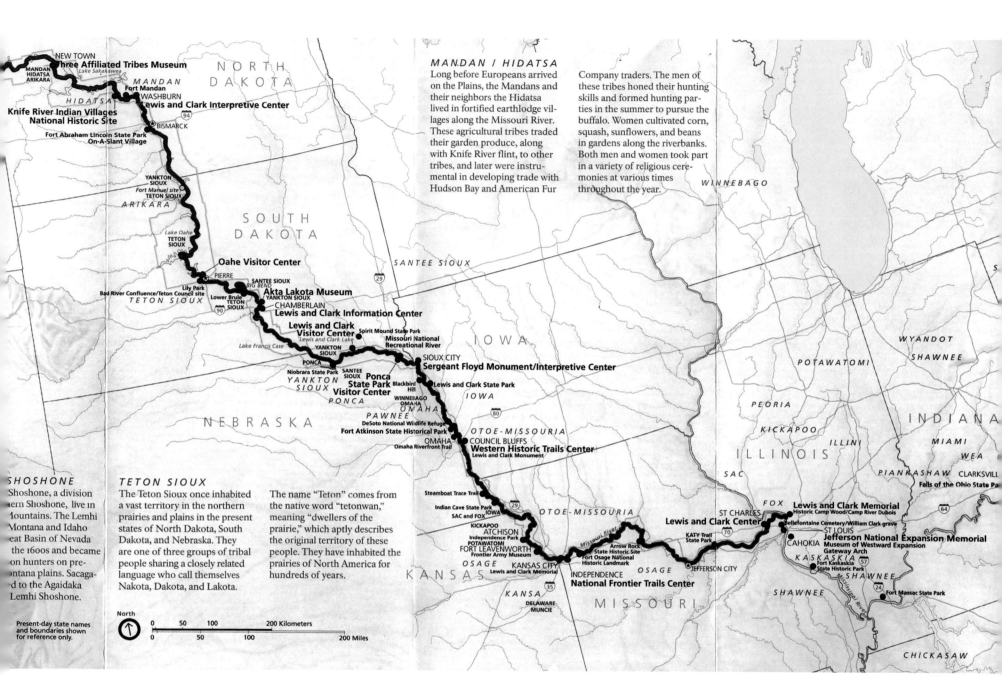

MANDAN / HIDATSA

Long before Europeans arrived on the Plains, the Mandans and their neighbors the Hidatsa lived in fortified earthlodge villages along the Missouri River. These agricultural tribes traded their garden produce, along with Knife River flint, to other tribes, and later were instrumental in developing trade with Hudson Bay and American Fur Company traders. The men of these tribes honed their hunting skills and formed hunting parties in the summer to pursue the buffalo. Women cultivated corn, squash, sunflowers, and beans in gardens along the riverbanks. Both men and women took part in a variety of religious ceremonies at various times throughout the year.

SHOSHONE

Shoshone, a division ...rn Shoshone, live in ...ountains. The Lemhi ...Montana and Idaho ...eat Basin of Nevada ... the 1600s and became ...n hunters on pre-...ntana plains. Sacaga-...d to the Agaidaka ...Lemhi Shoshone.

Present-day state names and boundaries shown for reference only.

TETON SIOUX

The Teton Sioux once inhabited a vast territory in the northern prairies and plains in the present states of North Dakota, South Dakota, and Nebraska. They are one of three groups of tribal people sharing a closely related language who call themselves Nakota, Dakota, and Lakota.

The name "Teton" comes from the native word "tetonwan," meaning "dwellers of the prairie," which aptly describes the original territory of these people. They have inhabited the prairies of North America for hundreds of years.

there is no service. You can drive for hours without seeing a gas station, and you can go for days without seeing a gourmet coffee emporium. On most of the route, the rivers or overland trails are followed by two-lane roads. Less of the trail is followed by interstate highways than gravel roads or no roads at all. It is amazing to travel this trail and realize how much of the American West is so little touched by the changes of the past two centuries.

We begin the Lewis and Clark Trail when it was just the kernel of an idea growing in the minds of President Thomas Jefferson and his secretary, Meriwether Lewis. We follow it as Lewis and Clark assembled their Corps of Discovery and as they set out on their epic trek across an 8,000-mile arc of the American heartland.

The Lewis and Clark trail along U.S. Highway 730 in Morrow County, Oregon. *Bill Yenne*

This is a Nez Perce tepee pitched in the Big Hole Valley of Montana. The hospitality afforded to Lewis and Clark by the Nez Perce played an important role in the success of their expedition. *Bill Yenne*

The rivers in the Rocky Mountains presented the Corps of Discovery with opportunities and challenges. Often they were so rough that traveling upstream was virtually impossible. However, when the Corps was able to travel downstream, such as on the Clearwater during the outbound trek, or on the Yellowstone during the return, they were able to move more quickly than would have been possible on the rugged shore. *Bill Yenne*

Chapter One

A Man and a Plan

Equal to the efforts of those who went on the expedition was the amazing vision of the man who initiated it. Few men command a larger presence in the annals of America's early years than Thomas Jefferson. Elected as the third president of the United States in 1800, Jefferson had been the principal author of the Declaration of Independence and was the secretary of state in George Washington's cabinet. More than a mere politician, Jefferson was a scientist, an accomplished architect, the founder of the University of Virginia, and one of the most widely respected political philosophers of his era.

This life portrait of Thomas Jefferson was painted by Charles Willson Peale from 1791 to 1792. *Independence NHP*

Meriwether Lewis was captured in this live portrait by Charles Willson Peale in 1807. *Independence NHP*

Jefferson was one of the truly brilliant men of American history. At an April 1962 White House dinner honoring Nobel laureates, President John F. Kennedy remarked that "I think this is the most extraordinary collection of talent, of human knowledge, that has ever been gathered together at the White House, with the possible exception of when Thomas Jefferson dined alone." Kennedy's quip clearly summarized Jefferson's legacy.

Jefferson's plan to explore the Missouri River headwaters and beyond was analogous to Kennedy's own audacious 1961 plan to send an American expedition to the moon. Both schemes represented extraordinary vision and required extraordinary courage. Both pushed the limits of American technological capability, and both were easily argued to be so impractical that it was virtually impossible. However, both expeditions succeeded, and both greatly expanded the limits of scientific knowledge.

Of course, both Jefferson and Kennedy were motivated as much by politics and economics as they were by science. For Kennedy, the Apollo program for American lunar landings was undertaken against the backdrop of competition with the Soviet Union, both on Earth and in outer space. For Jefferson, the Lewis and Clark Expedition would explore the Missouri and establish a de facto link between United States territory and the Pacific Coast, where the Spanish, British, and the Russians had outposts and commercial activities. Economically, access to this region meant access to the multimillion dollar international fur trade.

Jefferson was one of the first American leaders to imagine that the Pacific Northwest would be important to the new United States. By 1800, the importance of the Mississippi River was a given, and the eventual importance of the Missouri River could easily be predicted. In Jefferson's vision of the continent, the recently discovered Columbia River, thousands of miles away, was also potentially important to the United States. For three centuries, mariners had searched in vain for the mythical Northwest Passage, an all-weather water route between the Atlantic and the Pacific. If it could be found, it would revolutionize global commerce. Jefferson wondered whether the discovery of the Northwest Passage might be at hand.

The Columbia River, the largest river flowing into the Pacific from what is now the United States, had been known to exist for just a little more than a decade at that time. Because of a maze of islands and sandbars that disguise it, several British expeditions, including those of Captain James Cook and Captain George Vancouver, had sailed past the mouth of the Columbia River without ascertaining that there was a major river here. In 1788, Captain John Meares passed the mouth of the Columbia and reported that he was positive that no river flowed into the Pacific at this point. He even went so far as to name the bluff overlooking the mouth of the Columbia as "Cape Disappointment."

Finally, in 1792, the American sea captain, Robert Gray, found the mouth. He sailed past Cape Disappointment and into the great river that he named for his vessel, the *Columbia*. The cape was still known as "Disappointment" when Lewis and Clark arrived, and it still is today. The Corps of Discovery stood on the cape, but camped at an upstream point of land named for Gray.

Peale painted this live portrait of William Clark from 1807 to 1808.
Independence NHP

Jefferson was intrigued with the notion that the two great rivers flowing into the interior of the continent might serve as the basis for a more or less continuous waterway across the continent, the Northwest Passage. The headwaters of both the Missouri and the Columbia lay somewhere within the uncharted interior of the continent. How close they were was unknown, but in Jefferson's imagination, he could see explorers dragging a boat over a small rise from the headwaters of the Missouri to those of the Columbia. Nothing could be farther from the truth, but it would take an expedition to find out.

Although no one had yet crossed the breadth of what is now the United States, the Scottish explorer Alexander MacKenzie, an employee of the North West Company, had crossed what is now Canada, from Montreal to the Pacific Ocean, in 1793. MacKenzie's account of this trip was published in London in 1799, and this also greatly intrigued Jefferson.

It was here at Monticello, Thomas Jefferson's home in Virginia, that the president conceived of the grand scheme to explore the interior of the North American continent far beyond where any representative of the United States government had gone before.
Library of Congress

On January 18, 1803, President Jefferson requested money from Congress for a transcontinental scientific expedition from the United States—then entirely east of the Mississippi—to the Pacific. The idea was to send about a dozen men through territory claimed by Britain and France. To lead the expedition, the president picked U.S. Army Captain Meriwether Lewis, who then served as his personal secretary, a post roughly equivalent to what would be referred to today as White House chief of staff.

Born in Albemarle County, Virginia, on August 18, 1774, Lewis grew up not far from Jefferson's estate at Monticello and had known Jefferson most of his life. Lewis joined the U.S. Army in 1794 and quickly advanced to the rank of infantry captain within six years. To prepare Lewis for the task ahead, Jefferson arranged for him to learn celestial navigation and as much as possible about the geography and indigenous people west of the Mississippi. The president and the captain pored over MacKenzie's account of his 1793 trans-Canada trek using the maps in Jefferson's extensive personal collection.

Jefferson was anxious for geographical information about the vast unexplored continent and instructed Lewis to make frequent sextant readings of his latitude and longitude. The president armed Lewis with "instruments for ascertaining, by celestial observations, the geography of the country through which you will pass."

In March, Lewis commuted up to the U.S. Army arsenal at Harpers Ferry, Virginia, where he began to accumulate materiel for the trip, notably guns and ammunition, iron tomahawks, and other tools, including what Jefferson described as "light articles for barter and presents among the Indians."

Most notable of the captain's activities at the Virginia site (now part of West Virginia) was supervising the construction of a collapsible iron boat frame of his own design. As Jefferson and Lewis planned it, the expedition would travel by water as much as possible. At their mouths, both the Missouri and the Columbia were great, wide rivers that rivaled the scale of the Mississippi. However, Lewis was nagged by well-founded concerns that the rivers would be narrow at their source and that the boats used to start the trek would be fine for a while, but too wide as they reached the headwaters. He wanted to plan ahead and have a narrow boat available. His idea with the now-famous iron boat was that the frame could be folded down and carried until it was needed. It could then be unfolded and covered with hides in the field. His plan was to portage the unassembled boat over the Rocky Mountains, assemble it, and sail to the ocean.

From Harpers Ferry, Captain Lewis proceeded to Philadelphia, America's largest city, where Jefferson had arranged for him to be briefed by the nation's leading geographers, botanists, geologists, and scientists of other specialties. Also in Philadelphia, Lewis met with Jefferson's friend, Dr. Benjamin Rush, who provided him with medical advice and drugs. One of the leading physicians in America, Rush had been active in the American Revolution and was one of five physicians to have signed the Declaration of Independence. He was ahead of his time in his opposition to tobacco and his endorsement of alcohol in moderation, but he was very much an eighteenth-century man in his over-reliance on bloodletting as a cure for most ailments. Although Jefferson himself was skeptical of the practice, Rush convinced Lewis that it was a valuable practice, and the captain would spill the blood of his troops all too often as they crossed the continent.

On April 20, 1803, Meriwether Lewis wrote out this preliminary estimate of supplies that he thought would be essential to the success of the upcoming expedition. *Library of Congress*

This map of the Lewis and Clark trail across the western portion of North America from the Mississippi to the Pacific Ocean was prepared to accompany the 1814 edition of their journals. It was based on the original drawing by William Clark. *Library of Congress*

This handwritten memo from Thomas Jefferson to Meriwether Lewis, dated June 20, 1803, detailed the objectives that he hoped Lewis would accomplish on his expedition into the upper reaches of the Louisiana Purchase. *Library of Congress*

PERSONNEL OF THE CORPS OF DISCOVERY OFFICERS:

Captain Meriwether Lewis (1774–1809)
Captain (Second Lieutenant) William Clark (1770–1838)

CIVILIANS ATTACHED TO THE OFFICERS' MESS:
George Drouillard (?–1810) (a.k.a. Drewyer)
York (circa 1770–?)

SERGEANTS:
Sergeant Charles Floyd (1782–1804)
Sergeant Patrick Gass (1771–1870)
Sergeant John Ordway (circa 1775–1817)
Sergeant Nathaniel Hale Pryor (1772–1831)

CORPORAL:
Richard Warfington (1777–?)
(a.k.a. Warpenton, Worthington, or Wortheyton)

PRIVATES:
John Boley (?–?) (a.k.a. Boley or Boleye)
William E. Bratton (1778–1841) (a.k.a. Bratten)
John Collins (?–1823)
John Colter (circa 1775–1813)
Pierre Cruzatte (?–?) (a.k.a. Peter Cruzat)
John Dame (1784–?)
Joseph Field (circa 1772–1807) (a.k.a. Fields)
Reubin Field (circa 1771–1823?) (a.k.a. Fields)
Robert Frazer (?–1837) (a.k.a. Frazier or Frasure)
George Gibson (?–1809)
Silas Goodrich (?–1825?)
Hugh Hall (circa 1772–?)
Thomas Proctor Howard (1779–?)
Francois Labiche (?–?) (a.k.a. La Buish or Leebice)
Hugh McNeal (?–?)
John Newman (circa 1785–1838)
John Potts (1776–1808?)
Moses B. Reed (?–?)

John Robertson (circa 1780–?) (a.k.a. Roberson)
George Shannon (1785–1836)
John Shields (1769–1809)
John B. Thompson (?–1825?)
Ebenezer Tuttle (1773–?)
Peter M. Weiser (1781–?)
William Werner (?–?) (a.k.a. Warner)
Isaac White (circa 1774–?)
Joseph Whitehouse (circa 1775–?)
Alexander Hamilton Willard (1778–1865)
Richard Windsor (?–?) (a.k.a. Winser or Winsor)

CIVILIAN ENGAGÉS OR BOATMEN:
Jean Baptiste Deschamps (?–?) (the Patroon, or head boatman)
E. Cann (?–?) (a.k.a. Carr, Cane, or Carn)
Charles Caugee (?–?)
Joseph Collin (?–?)
Charles Hebert (?–?)
Jean Baptiste La Jeunesse (?–1806?) (a.k.a. La Guness or Lasones)
Joseph La Liberté (?–?) (a.k.a. Joseph La Bartee)
Etienne Malboeuf (circa 1775–?)
Peter Pinaut (circa 1776–?)
Paul Primeau (?–?) (a.k.a. Primaut, Preemau, or Premor)
Francois Rivet (circa 1757–1852) (a.k.a. Reevey)
Peter Roi (?–?)

CIVILIANS JOINING THE EXPEDITION AT FORT MANDAN IN 1805:
Toussaint Charbonneau (circa 1767–1843)
Sacagawea (circa 1787–1812) (a.k.a. Sakakawea or Sacajawea)
Jean Baptiste Charbonneau (1805–1866) (a.k.a. Pomp or Pompey)

Note: Some members of the Corps are extremely well documented in the journals of Lewis and Clark, while others are known only from brief passing references. The spellings of some names vary throughout the journals.

10 8

Harper's Ferry July 8th 1803.

Dear Sir,

The waggon which was employ-
:ed by Mr. Linnard the Military Agent
at Philadelphia, to transport the articles
forming my outfit, passed this place
on the 28th Ult. the waggoner deter-
:mined that his team was not suffi-
:ciently strong to take the whole of
the articles that had been prepared for
me at this place and therefore took
none of them; of course it became
necessary to provide some other means
of getting them forward; for this
purpose on the evening of the 5th
at Fredericktown
"engaged a person with a light two
horse waggon who promised to set out
with them this morning, in this however
he has disappointed me and I have
been

22973

In a moment of micromanagement, Jefferson advised Lewis to make several copies of his latitude and longitude observations, as well as of his other notes, and "Put into the care of the most trustworthy of your attendants to guard, by multiplying them against the accidental losses to which they will be exposed. A further guard would be, that one of these copies be on the cuticular membranes of the paper birch, as less liable to injury from damp tha common paper."

Jefferson was also anxious for ethnographic data on "the people inhabiting the line you will pursue." He instructed Lewis to "make yourself acquainted, as far as a diligent pursuit of your journey shall admit, with the names of the nations and their numbers; the extent and limits of their possessions; their relations with other tribes or nations; their language, traditions, monuments; their ordinary occupations in agriculture, fishing, hunting, war, arts, and the implements for these; their food, clothing, and domestic accommodations; the diseases prevalent among them, and the remedies they use; moral and physical circumstances which distinguish them from the tribes we know; peculiarities in their laws, customs, and dispositions; and articles of commerce they may need or furnish, and to what extent."

As would be the custom for the remainder of the century, bronze medallions known as "peace medals" that bore the likeness of the president were minted to be used as gifts for high-ranking members of the indigenous tribes with whom Lewis would meet in the interior.

Meriwether Lewis drafted this memo to President Thomas Jefferson on July 8, 1803, when he was at Harpers Ferry, Virginia (now West Virginia), and made his initial preparations for the expedition. *Library of Congress*

Little was known about the people living on the upper Missouri River. It was known that the Sioux was the principal tribe and that they dominated smaller tribes, such as the Oto, Omaha, Osage, Missouri, Pawnee, and Kansa. The Sioux controlled traffic along the Missouri River, exacting tribute both from the other tribes and the tiny handful of European trappers and traders that had been as far north as what are now the Dakotas. Farther north were the villages of the people of other tribes, who were reported by French and British traders and trappers to be more friendly to outsiders than the more powerful Sioux. These tribes were the Mandan, Arikara, and Hidatsa. The latter are also referred to as the Minitarre, a term that Lewis and Clark used with a variety of spellings. With these tribes in mind, Jefferson and Lewis tentatively planned for the expedition to spend the winter here before proceeding on to the Pacific.

If the information about these villages was scant, data about the area from there west was nonexistent. Between the villages and the Pacific, the nature of the indigenous population and the terrain were unknown, as was the distance itself. Nevertheless, it was hoped that the expedition could make it from the Mandan villages, to the Pacific, and back to St. Louis in one year.

Having conveyed the official marching orders, Jefferson concurred with Lewis' choice as a second in command for the expedition. It would be William Clark, under whom Lewis had served earlier in his military career.

Born on August 1, 1770, William was the younger brother of Revolutionary War hero and explorer George Rogers Clark. Although he was born in Virginia, Clark had grown up in Kentucky, which was then considered to be the western frontier. Living there, he had become a skilled woodsman. He joined the U.S. Army in 1792, served for four years, and attained the rank of captain. Lewis had served under him on the frontier in the army commanded by the legendary General "Mad" Anthony Wayne.

In June 1803, Lewis formally invited Clark to serve as co-captain on the expedition. Clark replied that "no man lives with whome I would perfur to undertake Such a Trip &c as your self."

Clark joined Lewis in August 1803 as preparations for the expedition were being made on the Ohio River, near the Falls of the Ohio at Louisville, but the paperwork reinstating him in the U.S. Army would not arrive until May 1804. Although Clark had left the U.S. Army as a captain and expected to be reinstated as such, his commission was as a lieutenant in the artillery. By then, there was no more time for paperwork, so Lewis and Clark simply decided to consider Clark as a captain, and he would be referred to as such throughout the expedition and in all of the journals and documents. The official designation of the expedition

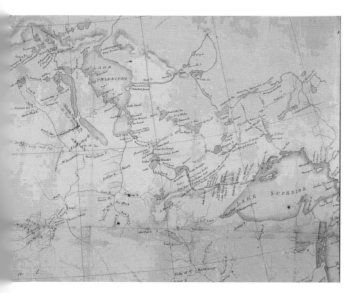

This provisional map of North America west of the Great Lakes by Nicholas King contains annotations made by Meriwether Lewis while he prepared for the expedition into the region. Note the vast empty swath between the Great Lakes and the Pacific. *Library of Congress*

A PARTIAL LISTING OF FOOD SUPPLIES CARRIED BY THE CORPS OF DISCOVERY FROM CAMP DUBOIS:

———— ◆◆◆ ————

(Sorted by weight)

24 Bags Natchies Corn, Hulled

50 bushels meal

1 Bag Coffee, 50 pounds

1 Keg of Hog's Lard, 100 pounds

1 Bag each of Beens and Pees, 100 pounds

2 Bags Sugar, 112 pounds

1 Bag of meal, 150 pounds

7 bags and four barrels of biscuit flour, 560 pounds

600 pounds of Grees

7 Barrels of Salt, each 750 pounds

11 Bags of Corn Hulled, each about 1,000 pounds

9 Bags of Common meal, each about 1,200 pounds

14 Bags of Parch meal, each about 1,200 pounds

30 half Barrels and three bags of flour, 3,400 pounds

50 Kegs of Pork, 3,705 pounds

Source: *The Food Journal of Lewis and Clark* by Mary Gunderson

In addition, the Corps of Discovery carried five barrels of whiskey, 193 pounds of portable soup, and 30 gallons of strong spirit wine.

ARMS & AMMUNITION

(A) Acquired by Lewis at Harpers Ferry:
(Sorted by count)
15 Rifles
15 Ball screws
15 Gun slings
15 Pairs of bullet molds
15 Wipers or gun worms
15 Powderhorns & pouches
24 Large knives
24 Pipe tomahawks
36 Pipe tomahawks for "Indian Presents"
40 Fish giggs
Extra parts of locks & tools for repairing arms

(B) Acquired en route to Camp Dubois:
1 pair Horseman's Pistols
1 Pair Pocket pistols
15 Scalping Knives and Belts
15 Cartouch Boxes
15 painted Knapsacks
15 Gun Slings
15 Powder Horns & Pouches—From Public Store
15 Powder Horns
18 Tomahawks
30 Brushes & Wires
50 pounds of Best rifle Powder
52 leaden Canisters for Gunpowder
125 Musket Flints
176 Pounds of Gun powder
200 Rifle Flints
420 Pounds of Sheet Lead

No mention of Dr. Rush in the context of the expedition is complete without mention of the notorious Rush's Pills, of which Lewis and Clark carried 50 dozen. Better known as "thunderclappers" for their laxative properties, they were the doctor's own creation as a treatment for maladies that did not require bloodletting. They contained a laxative, as well as Calomel, which was six parts mercury to one part chlorine, that acted as a purgative. In short, Rush and the medical establishment believed that the body could be cured of most ailments by purging or draining bodily fluids. The mercury, which is now obviously known to be toxic, was then widely prescribed—and apparently quite effective—as a treatment for venereal disease. The deadly long-term effects were unknown.

Also in Philadelphia, Lewis obtained nearly 200 pounds of a substance known as "portable soup." An early precursor to canned food or military K-rations, portable soup was a ration concocted from boiled and concentrated meat and vegetables placed into containers (just add water). Portable, but later determined to be barely palatable, it was to be mixed and boiled with water for emergency use.

Even as Lewis made the rounds of the salons of the Philadelphia scientists, events across the Atlantic would abruptly change the complexion of his trip to the Pacific. In Paris, Jefferson's minister to France, Robert Livingston, along with Jefferson's special envoy, James Monroe (later the fifth president of the United States), had been in negotiations with the government of Napoleon Bonaparte to purchase the city of New Orleans at the mouth of the Mississippi River, along with West Florida (today the southern parts of the states of Alabama and Mississippi).

In April 1803, Livingston, Monroe, and Jefferson were made an offer they could not refuse. Suddenly, in the midst of discussions, French Foreign Minister Charles Maurice de Tallyrand stunned them by proposing to sell the United States all of Louisiana, and not just New Orleans and West Florida.

Before 1803, "Louisiana" meant a region more than 18 times larger than the size of the state today. Claimed by France in 1682, the area was defined as all of the area drained by the Mississippi and Missouri rivers and their tributaries. When France lost the Seven Years War in 1763, the part of Louisiana east of the Mississippi was ceded to Britain, and the part to the west went to Spain. When the United States won its Revolutionary War against Britain in 1783, it inherited the land to the east of the river, and in 1800, Spain ceded the area to the west back to France. The latter transaction was short-lived. By 1803, Napoleon viewed the vast, mostly land-locked Louisiana as more of a liability than an asset.

In 1803, Napoleon had his plate full with his activities in Europe. In the Western Hemisphere, his troops were embroiled in a difficult war in Haiti. Meanwhile, in the Mississippi valley, American traders outnumbered both the French and Spanish, and it seemed inevitable that the river would become an American highway. To Napoleon, the expedient thing to do was to sell Louisiana to the Americans rather than wait and have them take it. For Thomas Jefferson, there was no question of whether to make the deal. The treaty concluding the transaction was signed at the end of April 1803 and was ratified by the Senate in October, but the official hand-over did not occur until the following spring.

These reproduction items represent some of the weapons and supplies Meriwether Lewis acquired at the Harpers Ferry Armory in 1803 for the expedition. *NPS photo by Marsha Wassel*

The Louisiana Purchase essentially doubled the territory of the United States. For a total of $15 million, the country added about 820,000 square miles. In fact, at the time, nobody was exactly sure how much territory had been added because the area of Louisiana had yet to be surveyed.

Prior to 1803, the Spanish had shown little interest in Louisiana, and only a tiny handful of French or British trappers had traveled up the Missouri as far as present-day North Dakota. Even less was known about the Columbia River far to the northwest. It was time to know all of this territory, and Jefferson already had his plan in motion.

With the Louisiana Purchase finalized, Jefferson was able to obtain documents from the French ambassador that would guarantee safe passage for Lewis through the territory from any French citizens that were not yet aware of the transfer of title. He was also able to obtain the same from Britain's ambassador. Spain, meanwhile, actually sent troops to try and intercept Lewis and Clark, but they never got remotely close to where Lewis and Clark traveled.

Jefferson also supplied Lewis with open letters of credit, authorizing him to obtain any supplies necessary from "the consuls, agents, merchants, or citizens of any nation with which we have intercourse, assuring them, in our name, that any aids they may furnish you shall be honourably repaid, and on demand."

On June 30, 1803, Lewis received his official orders from the president. Jefferson formally explained in writing that, "The object of your mission is to explore the Missouri River, and such principal streams of it, as, by its course and communication with the waters of the Pacific Ocean."

Betraying his eagerness for the discovery of the elusive Northwest Passage, Jefferson told Lewis, "The interesting points of the portage between the heads of the Missouri, and of the water offering the best communication with the Pacific ocean, should also be fixed by observation; and the course of that water to the ocean, in the same manner as that of the Missouri."

This is a detail of the flintlock mechanism of a 1792 military-issue rifle like Lewis acquired at the Harpers Ferry Armory for use by the Corps of Discovery. The flintlock works on the principal of snapping a piece of flint against steel to spark an explosion in the powder charge rammed into the barrel. *NPS photo from Harpers Ferry Center*

Captain Meriwether Lewis supervises the loading of his supply wagon at Harpers Ferry in July 1803. He left for Pittsburgh, Pennsylvania, on July 8, and the loaded wagon followed the next day. *National Park Service, Harpers Ferry Center, artist Keith Rocco*

In this illustration by Keith Rocco, Harpers Ferry Armory superintendent Joseph Perkins and Captain Meriwether Lewis (right) inspect the assembled iron boat frame. Designed by Lewis, the craft comprised an iron frame that detached in sections and a leather covering that stretched around it. He imagined that a light boat of this kind would be needed when the Missouri River got too shallow for the heavy wooden boats to navigate. The Armory mechanics assigned to the project had considerable difficulty assembling the iron frame, and Lewis was forced to prolong his Harpers Ferry stay from the week he had planned to more than a month. *National Park Service, Harpers Ferry Center, artist Keith Rocco*

would be the U.S. Army Corps of Volunteers of North Western Discovery, better known simply as the Corps of Discovery. Just as Britain's great navigators, such as Captain James Cook, explored the world's oceans under the banner of the Royal Navy, the United States sent its official expedition into the interior of the continent under the banner and military discipline of the U.S. Army. The Army of 1803 consisted of two regiments of infantry, one regiment of artillery, a small corps of engineers, and the newly developed Corps of Discovery. The men of the new organization were drawn from all three of the line regiments.

The initial plan of a fast trip with a dozen men would grow to an expedition involving nearly four times that number and three fairly large river-going vessels. The idea of starting the trek in the summer of 1803 would also elude the grasp of Lewis and his co-captain.

Lewis had placed an order for a keelboat to be built to his specifications in Pittsburgh. Located at the point where the Ohio River begins at the confluence of the Allegheny and Monongahela, the city was then the center of riverboat building in the United States.

The keelboat, or barge, as it was referred to by Lewis and Clark, was 55 feet long. Its beam, or width, was 8 feet, 4 inches, making it somewhat narrower than most similar craft of this length. This was further evidence of Lewis' concern regarding the width of the river or its channels in the unknown sections far upstream. The keelboat was designed to be propelled by a sail or rowed 20 double-banked oars with a 16-foot sweep. In practice, however, it would be poled or pulled from shore.

The vessel was armed with a single cannon, or "bow pece," though the exact details of the gun are not known. During the winter of 1804–1805, it was taken ashore and mounted within Fort Mandan.

Unfortunately, the boatbuilder that Lewis picked to construct his keelboat was several weeks behind schedule, and Lewis feared that he would not be able to get down the Ohio River to the Mississippi River—much less up the Missouri—before winter set in.

Meanwhile, Clark traveled to Louisville to recruit a team of young Kentucky frontiersmen for the Corps of Discovery.

CONTENTS OF THE 21 BALES OF LIGHT ARTICLES FOR BARTER & PRESENTS AMONG THE INDIANS:

(Sorted by count)

1 Trunk to pack sundry Indian Presents	24 Red striped tapes
1 Half catty, India S. Silk	24 None-so-pretty
1 Pair of Red flannel 47.5 yards	24 Earrings
1 Box with 100 larger Bells	33 Lockets
2 Pounds of Vermillion	42 Tinsel Bands, assorted
2 Cards Beads	48 Calico Ruffled Shirts
2 Corn Mills	48 Butcher Knives
3 Pounds of Beads	66 Fancy 1 Floss
6 Papers Small Bells	72 Rings
6.5 Pounds of Strips Sheet Iron	73 Bunches Beads, assorted
8 Pounds of Red lead	96 Burning Looking Glasses
8 Brass Kettles at four per pound	144 Striped silk ribbons
8.5 Pounds of Red Beads	144 Iron Combs
10 Pounds of Brads	144 Pocket Looking Glasses
11 Pairs of Handkerchiefs, assorted	130 Tobacco (pigtail)
12 Pounds of Brass Strips	132 Knives
12 Pounds of Brass Wire	180 Scissors
12 Pipe Tomahawks	180 Pewter Looking Glasses
12 Ivory Combs	288 Thimbles, assorted
12 Needle Cases	432 Curtain Rings
14 Pounds of Knitting pins	500 Broaches
15 Blankets (from Public Store)	864 Binding
21 Pounds of Thread, assorted	1,152 Seat or Moccasin Awls
22 Yards of Scarlet Cloth	2,800 Fishhooks, assorted
	4,600 Needles, assorted

The International Fur Exchange in St. Louis, across the Mississippi from the Camp Dubois replica in Hartford, Illinois, is identified as a landmark on the Lewis and Clark trail. When the trail was opened in 1920, St. Louis had been the crossroads of the American fur trade for 150 years. Thanks to the information brought back by Lewis and Clark in 1806, trappers were able to exploit the beaver population on the upper Missouri River. Today, the beavers live on, but the trappers have faded into history. *Bill Yenne*

A PARTIAL LISTING OF CAMP EQUIPAGE CARRIED BY THE CORPS OF DISCOVERY FROM CAMP DUBOIS:

(Sorted by count)

1 Corn Mill
1 Packing Hogshead (from Public Store)
1 Block tin Sauce pan
1 Rule
1 Sett Iron Weights
1 Tin Box sqr. Of Small art.
1 Shoe float
1 Pound Sealing Wax (from Public Store)
1 Saw Sett
1 Common Tent (from Public Store)
1 Whetstone
1 Stand of Fishing Lines With hooks (Complete)
1 Set of Gold Scales and Weights
1 Sportsman's flask
2 Tin Lanthorns
2 Tin Lamps
2 Pair Large Shears
2 Pair Pliers
2 Small Vises
2 P. Pocket steel yards
2 Adzes
2 Hatchets
2 Hand Saws
4 Tin Horns
4 Drawing Knives
6 Papers Ink Powder (from Public Store)

6 Augers
6 Brass Kettles & Porterage
6 Brass Inkstands (from Public Store)
8 Tents (Bought by the Purveyor of Richard Wevill)
8 Ps. Cat gut for Mosquito Curtain
8 Receipt Books (from Public Store)
9 Chisels
12 Pounds Castile Soap
15 Small cord
24 Table Spoons
36 Pint Tumblers
36 Gimblets
45 Bags (Bought by the Purveyor of Richard Wevill)
48 Ps. Tape (from Public Store)
48 Packages Needles and large Awls
100 Quills (from Public Store)
125 Large fishing Hooks
204 Files and Rasps
Fishing Lines, assorted
10 yards of Country Linen, Oiled (Bought by the Purveyor of Richard Wevill)
20 yards of Brown Linen, Oiled (Bought by the Purveyor of Richard Wevill)

Clark also acquired sheets of lead from Kentucky's Olive Mine to make shot for the muskets and sinkers for fishing line.

By mid-October, Lewis arrived at Louisville and hired a local boatman to guide the new keelboat safely through the rapids known as the Falls of the Ohio. During the coming weeks, Lewis and Clark enlisted the first members of the Corps of Discovery, the so-called "Nine Young Men from Kentucky." They were sergeants Charles Floyd and Nathaniel Pryor, along with privates William Bratton, John Colter, Joseph and Reubin Field, George Gibson, George Shannon, and John Shields. Also in the Corps by this time was Clark's "body servant" (his personal slave), an African-American man named York.

As the keelboat made its way downstream from Louisville, additional men were added to the Corps of Discovery. At Fort Massac in southern Illinois Territory, two U.S. Army privates, John Newman and Joseph Whitehouse, volunteered for the Corps. Another civilian

Today, the massive westward migration that was inspired by Lewis and Clark is memorialized in the Gateway Arch, which is located on the Mississippi Riverfront in St. Louis. The 630-foot stainless steel arch was designed by architect Eero Saarinen during a nationwide competition in 1947 and 1948 and was constructed between 1963 and 1965. It is seen as a monument to the spirit of the western pioneers. *Bill Yenne*

volunteer was George Drouillard, an expert hunter and guide of Shawnee and French descent who was widely versed in native languages and could act as a French translator. Referred to in the Lewis and Clark journals as "Drewyer," Drouillard turned out to be perhaps the single most important man—other than the co-captains—on the expedition.

When the keelboat reached the Mississippi and turned upstream toward the mouth of the Missouri, it became obvious that more men would be needed to propel the boat against the current on the two rivers. As they had made their plans, Jefferson and Lewis knew that the Corps of Discovery would have to travel upstream on the Mississippi and the Missouri, but neither had a practical grasp of exactly how physically difficult it would be to fight the powerful currents of the two rivers. Nothing about the Potomac or other Eastern rivers had prepared Lewis for what lay ahead.

On November 29, they stopped at Fort Kaskaskia, near Ellis Grove, Illinois, which was the U.S. Army post farthest west in the United States and farthest north on the Mississippi River. Here, additional volunteers joined the Corps of Discovery from the 1st Infantry Regiment. They included Sergeant John Ordway and privates Peter Weiser, Richard Windsor, Patrick Gass, John Boley, and John Collins. Five U.S. Army artillery privates who also joined at Fort Kaskaskia were John Dame, John Robertson, Ebenezer Tuttle, Isaac White, and Alexander Hamilton Willard.

Winter had already set in by the time the Corps of Discovery finally reached St. Louis on the morning of December 11, 1803. The Corps discovered that the official transfer of the Louisiana Purchase had not yet occurred, so Lewis and Clark were obliged to put the men into winter quarters across the river in Illinois Territory. The ceremony marking the formal transfer of the Louisiana Purchase to the United States would not occur in St. Louis until March 1804, nearly three months later.

While Lewis debarked from the keelboat to make arrangements for supplies in St. Louis, Clark traveled about 18 miles upriver to a place opposite the mouth of the Missouri River and near a smaller stream flowing into the Mississippi from Illinois. The stream was known to the Americans as Wood River; the French called it *Riviere a Dubois*. Here, the Corps of Discovery made the first encampment of the expedition at Camp Dubois, or Camp River Dubois.

Completed by Christmas Eve in 1803, Camp Dubois was the Corps' home for nearly five months. During this time, Clark instituted a strict code of discipline as he began the task of molding the Corps into a cohesive military unit. Meanwhile, Lewis spent most of the winter at Cahokia, Illinois, directly across the Mississippi from St. Louis, or in the city of St. Louis, making the final arrangements for supplies and provisions. Additional personnel were recruited into the Corps of Discovery during the early months of 1804, and these men were formally enlisted at Camp Dubois at the end of March. By this time, Clark noticed that the buds were starting to appear on the trees around Camp Dubois, and the Corps of Discovery was anxious to get underway, but the co-captains were cautiously waiting for the fast current of the Missouri, fed by the spring thaw upstream, to slacken. Early in May, they began river trials of the three boats that they would take upstream. In addition to the keelboat, they took a pair of pirogues, large open-topped boats similar in size and appearance to

The Jefferson National Expansion Memorial includes the Gateway Arch and the Museum of Westward Expansion, which is located underground below the arch. The museum contains exhibits and artifacts that relate to the Lewis and Clark Expedition and to the natural history of the 11 states they passed through after they left the St. Louis area.
Bill Yenne

ocean-going whaleboats. One of these is referred to in the journals of Lewis and Clark as the Red Pirogue, the other as the White Pirogue. The Red Pirogue had been acquired the previous year on the Ohio River between Pittsburgh and Louisville, and the White Pirogue was added to the expedition at Fort Kaskaskia.

Finally, after several weather delays, William Clark gave the word. On May 14, 1804, he wrote in his journal, "Set out from Camp River a Dubois at 4 oClock P.M. and proceded up the Missouris under Sail to the first Island in the Missouri and Camped on the upper point opposit a Creek on the South Side below a ledge of limestone rock Called Colewater, made 4 1/2 miles, the Party Consisted of 2, Self one frenchman [Drouillard] and 22 Men in the Boat of 20 ores, 1 Serjt. & 7 french in a large Perogue, a Corp and 6 Soldiers in a large Perogue."

Clark noted that it was "A Cloudy rainey day," but added, "Men in high Spirits."

Chapter Two

The Trail Begins

L ewis and Clark's 8,000-mile journey began with a single step, and that step was taken as the men boarded their flagship and the two pirogues at Camp Dubois on May 14, 1804. The first step was taken by Clark. Lewis was in St. Louis and did not join the expedition until the following day at St. Charles, Missouri. As Clark wrote, "I determined to go as far as St. Charles a french Village 7 Leags. up the Missourie, and wait at that place untill Capt. Lewis Could finish the business in which he was obliged to attend to at St Louis and join me by Land from that place 24 miles."

This view looks across the Missouri River from Iowa to Nebraska at Milepost 488 from Camp Dubois, near the town of Bartlett, Iowa. Storm clouds are starting to gather in the west. *Bill Yenne*

The Lewis and Clark expedition began at a humble fortification known as *Camp Dubois* or *Camp River Dubois*. It was completed by Christmas Eve in 1803 and was the home of the Corps of Discovery for nearly five months. This reconstruction, located in Hartford, Illinois, is within a few miles of the original site, which is now probably beneath the shifting waters of the Mississippi. *Bill Yenne*

Today, Milepost 1 on the Lewis and Clark Trail is the Lewis and Clark Interpretive Center at the western end of New Pogue Road in Hartford, Illinois. Opened in time for the 2004 bicentennial, the 14,000-square-foot facility is on the site of Lewis and Clark State Park, originally established in the 1950s on the Illinois shore that faces the confluence of the Mississippi and Missouri rivers. Administered by the Illinois Historic Preservation Agency, it includes a 55-foot full-scale replica of the keelboat, other exhibits, and the Convergence Theater, where a film about Lewis and Clark is shown. A full-scale replica of Camp Dubois is outside the modern visitors center. Because of changes in the courses of the rivers over the intervening two centuries, the actual site of the camp is calculated to be beneath the Mississippi River, but the replica fort is thought to be within a few miles of the original.

St. Charles, Missouri, where Lewis joined Clark on the second day, is thought by some to be a worthy consideration as an alternate to Camp Dubois as an official starting point of the Corps of Discovery expedition. It is located at Milepost 27, by way of Illinois State Route 3 and Interstate 270 from Camp Dubois, or Missouri State Route 94, which begins across the Mississippi from Alton, Illinois. Today, the Lewis and Clark Center in St. Charles features many exhibits that interpret the voyage, including hand-painted dioramas of scenes from the trek. A replica keelboat was built here and launched in 2004 for a re-enactment of the expedition. St. Charles is also the trailhead to the Katy Trail, which follows the route of the old Missouri-Kansas-Texas (MKT) Railroad, which was known informally as the Katy because of the last two letters of its initials. The Katy Trail is a Missouri State Park that follows 185 miles of the Lewis and Clark Trail along the Missouri River from St. Charles to Sedalia.

The main highway route of the Lewis and Clark Trail west of St. Charles is State Route 94 as far as the Missouri State Capitol at Jefferson City and State Route 179 to Boonville. Jefferson City, which is Milepost 138 from Camp Dubois, was not a city in 1804 and is not mentioned as such by Lewis and Clark in early June 1804.

Also conspicuous in its absence is mention of the legendary frontiersman Daniel Boone, who was living on the Missouri River near the mouth of Femme Osage River at the present town of Defiance, about 20 river miles west of St. Charles. A summit conference between Boone, Lewis, and Clark became one of the great missed opportunities of history as the Corps of Discovery passed almost within sight of Boone's home on or about May 23.

Two days into the trip west, averaging a little more than three miles a day, they reached what Clark described as the "Small french Village called La Charatt of five families only, in the bend to the Starbord This is the Last Settlement of Whites."

Pushing the boats upstream against the current in the Missouri River during the summer and fall of 1804 was far more difficult than traveling with the current two years later. In 1804, three miles a day was not uncommon. The trip downstream on the Missouri in 1806 was much faster. It was in this vicinity that Clark made note on September 19, 1806, of "Haveing Came 72 miles."

The first immigrant wagon trains across the nation's midsection followed the Missouri River and Lewis and Clark from St. Louis to Independence to Kansas City. The first railroads across the American heartland followed these wagon ruts.

In western Missouri, U.S. Highway 24 provides the closest views of the Missouri River, crossing it at Waverly and following it south into the Kansas City metropolitan area. Interstate 70 cuts a much straighter path than could have been imagined by those generations of pioneers.

Moments after crossing the state line between Kansas City, Missouri, and Kansas City, Kansas, Highway 24 crosses the Lewis and Clark Viaduct at the Kansas River, which enters the Missouri River at this point. This confluence marks Milepost 333 by the highway and was noted by Clark on June 29, 1804, as having been "366 miles above the mouth of Missouri."

Inside the reconstructed Camp Dubois is a re-creation of the room where William Clark may have dined. For most of the winter of 1803–1804, he dined alone, while Meriwether Lewis was across the Mississippi in St. Louis or elsewhere. The replica fort is in Hartford, Illinois, and is adjacent to the Lewis and Clark Interpretive Center. *Bill Yenne*

Clark also noted that this was "A verry bad place of water," and that the "Sturn of the [Keel]boat Struck a moveing Sand & turned within 6 Inches of a large Sawyer, if the Boat had Struck the Sawyer, her Bow must have been Knocked off & in Course She must hav Sunk in the Deep water below." He concluded by noting that the exhausted Corps of Discovery "Came to & camped on the [south side] late in the evening."

It was also on June 29, at the mouth of the Kansas, that two corpsmen were court-martialed. John Collins was charged "with getting drunk on his post this morning out of whiskey put under his Charge as a Sentinal and for Suffering Hugh Hall to draw whiskey out of the Said Barrel intended for the party." Hall was charged with "takeing whiskey out of a Keg . . . Contrary to all order, rule, or regulation." Both men were found guilty and whipped.

By the end of June 1804, the Corps of Discovery was beginning to see the sizable numbers of wildlife that would be reported as the expedition made its way across the Great Plains. On that busy day of June 29, Clark made note of "Many Deer Killed to day," and the following day, he mentioned that he "Saw a verry large wolf on the Sand bar this morning walking near a gange of Turkeys," and that the expedition "Killed 2 Deer Bucks."

In 1808, Clark returned to design and build Fort Osage near here. It remained as the westernmost United States government presence until 1818. A reconstruction of this fort is located at Sibley, Missouri, just east of the edge of the Kansas City metropolitan area between Highway 24 and the Missouri River.

In 1804, the future site of Kansas City was beyond the edge of civilization as the Corps knew it. By 1806, things had changed. They were meeting boats nearly every day in these waters. On September 16, 1806, "At 10 AM we met a large tradeing perogue bound for the [Pawnees]. . . at 11 AM we met young Mr. Bobidoux with a large boat of six ores and 2 Canoes."

The next day, the Corps of Discovery met "Captain McClellin late a Capt. of Artily of the U States Army assending in a large boat." At that time, the captain was on what Clark referred to as a "Reather a speculative expedition to the confines of New Spain, with the view to entroduce a trade with those people." His expedition is one

A cooking fire smolders within the stockade of the Camp Dubois replica. The cooking vessels, colorfully referred to as "kittles" by Lewis and Clark, are typical of the early nineteenth century, as is the ax seen in the background.
Bill Yenne

The bunks within the reconstructed Camp Dubois are thought to be similar to those used by the Corps' enlisted men during the winter of 1803–1804. *Mike Stout, Lewis and Clark Interpretive Center*

of the little-known early efforts by the United States government to survey the area due west of Kansas City.

They turned north from Kansas City. The river flows generally from west to east across the state of Missouri, but at the mouth of the Kansas River there is an abrupt turn and the trail that follows the Missouri upriver angles north by northwest nearly to Canada before it turns west again. This is the direction taken by the Corps of Discovery through the end of 1804.

Missouri State Route 45 follows the river and the Lewis and Clark Trail out of Kansas City and reaches the town of Lewis and Clark, Missouri, near Lewis and Clark Lake and Lewis and Clark State Park, and all are at or near Milepost 375. It was here that the Corps of Discovery spent July 4, 1804. As Clark observed, they "Ussered in the day by a discharge of one shot from our Bow piece." In honor of the day, Lewis and Clark agreed to name the small stream that entered the Missouri, from what is now Kansas, as Independence Creek.

Clark also noted that the lake that was later named after him and his co-captain "Is clear and Contain great quantities of fish and Gees & Goslings, The great quantity of those fowl in this Lake induce me to Call it the Gosling Lake."

He went on to describe the area colorfully and observed that "As we approached this place the Praree had a most butifull appearance. Hills & Valies interspsd with Coops of Timber gave a pleasing deversity to the Senery . . . the right fork of Creek Independence Meandering thro the middle of the Plain a point of high Land near the river givs an allivated Situation. At this place the Kanzas Indians formerley lived. this Town [the former village of the Kansa people]

The re-enactor portraying Captain William Clark stands in the doorway of the reconstruction of Clark's quarters at Camp Dubois. These accommodations, while a cut above those of the enlisted men, were still quite spartan. *Mike Stout, Lewis and Clark Interpretive Center*

This drawing by Richard Guthrie provides an excellent overview of the design of the Camp Dubois replica fort. Clark's journals provide only a few details about the original fort's design and construction, so the replica is based on a study of fortifications that were built on the frontier by the U.S. Army in similar locations around the turn of the nineteenth century. *Lewis and Clark Interpretive Center*

appears to have covd. a large Space, the nation must have been noumerous at the time they lived here." The Independence Day festivities were concluded with "An extra Gill of whiskey."

Today, U.S. Highway 59 crosses the Missouri from Atchison, Kansas, at this point and proceeds north. Between Atchison and St. Joseph, Missouri, this highway is the closest road that runs parallel to the Missouri River.

On July 6, the Corps of Discovery was about 8 miles north of Independence Creek when Sergeant Floyd noted in his journal that there was a "Jentell Brees from the South west." Today, his misspelling is memorialized in the naming of the location as the Jentell Brees Access. About 4 miles west of U.S. Highway 59, this access site for boaters wishing to place their craft into the Missouri is maintained by the Missouri Department of Conservation. The Corps passed this away again on September 13, 1806.

Milepost 1 on the Lewis and Clark trail is at the Lewis and Clark Interpretive Center in Hartford, Illinois. The Corps of Discovery started from this point on May 14, 1804. Administered by the Illinois Historic Preservation Agency, the Interpretive Center contains the Convergence Theater, where a film about the expedition is shown. *Bill Yenne*

This 55-foot full-scale replica of the Lewis and Clark expedition flagship is located within the Lewis and Clark Interpretive Center at Hartford, Illinois. The vessel was equipped with a sail, but oar-locks were also provided for rowing. *Bill Yenne*

In 1804, moving upstream, they were seven weeks away from St. Charles. Two years later, moving with the current, they covered the same distance in just eight days.

The future site of St. Joseph, Missouri, was passed by the Corps of Discovery on July 7, 1804, and later played an important role in the history of the American West as the jumping off point for many wagon trains. It is here that the memories of Lewis and Clark blend with the ethos of the westward migration that occurred in the century that followed their journey. St. Louis styles itself as the gateway to the West, but the real jumping off point was on the western side of the state of Missouri. The Pony Express, that signature institution of the westward migration, had its eastern terminus here. Inaugurating service to Sacramento, California, in 1860, the Pony Express riders managed the trip in less than two weeks, which is about the same length of time one might travel today by following the back roads and stopping frequently at points of interest.

North of St. Joseph, the Missouri River officially follows U.S. Highway 59 and State Route 111, but from this point north to Sioux City, Iowa, Interstate 29 is as close to the

This cutaway view of the Lewis and Clark flagship replica at the Lewis and Clark Interpretive Center at Hartford, Illinois, shows how supplies were packed beneath the deck. Barrels contained everything from salt pork to whiskey. The metal cans contained "portable soup," a concoction of boiled and concentrated meat and vegetables. *Bill Yenne*

We know from the journals that the bridge of Lewis and Clark's flagship was covered with a canvas sun shade. The vessel's armament included a pair of blunderbusses that were mounted here, as well as a cannon on the bow. These were never fired in anger, but they came close to being used during a confrontation with the Lakota in September 1804. *Bill Yenne*

Missouri as any of the smaller roads and is officially marked with signs describing it as the Lewis and Clark Trail. An alternate is U.S. Highway 75 on the Nebraska side of the Missouri River, but it is no closer to the river than the interstate. The Nebraskans have memorialized the sojourn of the captains by naming this section of Highway 75 as the Lewis and Clark Scenic Byway.

Milepost 464 marks the border between Missouri and Iowa. Before they had reached this point, Lewis and Clark passed several outposts of familiar "civilization." Beyond here, there were none. On the outbound trek in 1804, it took the Corps of Discovery two months of strenuous pulling and poling to reach this point. On their inbound journey two years later, the distance to St. Charles was more on the order of two weeks. Today, a casual car trip takes about two days.

Because of the broad flood plain of the Missouri, however, the roads are generally several miles away and the river is sporadically in view. Crossings, such as the one on Iowa State Route 2 that leads from Interstate 29 across to Nebraska City, Nebraska, provide a good view of the Missouri as it meanders through this flood plain.

As they made their way north along the southern section of the Missouri River that now forms the border between Nebraska and Iowa, the co-captains made note of the features that today make this area the true agricultural heartland of the United States. On July 5, they observed "Great quant[itie]s of Grapes, berries & roses." On July 12, it was noted that "Thickets of Plumbs Cher[ri]es &c are Seen on [the river's] banks." Clark noted, "I got grapes on the banks nearly ripe, observed great quantities, of Grapes, plums Crab apls and a Wild Cherry resembling the Common Wild Cherry, only larger." On July 14, there were "Plumbs of different kinds, Grapes, and Goose berries," and the following day, Clark "Saw Great quantities of Grapes, Plums, wild Cherries of 2 Kinds, Hazelnuts, and Goosberries."

In the journals, mention was made almost daily of the success of the hunting parties who worked the surrounding plains as the Corps strained to push the boats up the river. On July 19, Clark remarked that breakfast had been "Rosted Ribs of a Deer." Although the wildlife are no longer as plentiful on these shores as they were two centuries ago, the river still boasts sizable numbers of catfish, another delicacy the Corps of Discovery ate as they made their way north.

These tools on display at the Lewis and Clark Interpretive Center in Hartford, Illinois, are typical of the early nineteenth century. The hammer, adze, and chisel were tools used to build and furnish their winter quarters and to make repairs. The adzes were essential to build the canoes that were necessary in 1805 and 1806. *Bill Yenne*

This view of the cutaway Lewis and Clark flagship replica at the Lewis and Clark Interpretive Center at Hartford, Illinois, shows the captains' accommodations aboard the vessel. *Bill Yenne*

Captain William Clark is the centerpiece of this view of the interior of the Lewis and Clark Interpretive Center at Hartford, Illinois. *David Blachette, Lewis and Clark Interpretive Center*

Lewis and Clark took a variety of goods to trade with the American Indians they expected to meet during the expedition. These items included hatchets, beads, and tools. These replicas are on display at the Lewis and Clark Interpretive Center in Hartford, Illinois. *Mike Stout, Lewis and Clark Interpretive Center*

In terms of their mandate to study the zoology of the region, the captains made note of the wildlife they hunted, as well as the presence of beaver and other creatures. They were particularly intrigued by the badger, with which they were not familiar. They carefully described it as "An Anamale Called by the French 'Brarow' (actually *blaireau*), and by the [Pawnees] 'Cho-car-tooch.' This Anamale Burrows in the Ground and feeds on Flesh, Bugs, & vigatables. His Shape & Size is like that of a Beaver, his head mouth &c. is like a Dogs with Short Ears, his Tail and Hair like that of a Ground Hog, and longer, and lighter. his Interals like the interals of a Hog . . . his Skin thick and loose, his Belly is White and the Hair Short. A white Streek from his nose to his Sholders." They skinned the badger and prepared its pelt to be sent back to Jefferson.

Despite the abundance of fruit and game, all was not a bed of wild roses. On July 12, Alexander Willard was "brought forward" and court martialed for "Lying down and Sleeping on his post whilst a Sentinal, on the night of the 11th." For this infraction, as the Corps of Discovery moved into Sioux country, the private was sentenced to receive "One hundred lashes on his bear back."

Although the Sioux had yet to be encountered, the Corps was engaged with almost constant warfare with a smaller nemesis. As Clark noted on July 17, "A puff of wind brought Swarms of Misquitors, which disapeared in two hours, blown off by a Continuation of the Same brees." On July 27, Clark said that the evening would have been "verry agreeable, had the Misquiters been tolerably Pacifick, but thy were rageing all night,

Tom Schlafly's Saint Louis Brewery created the Lewis and Clark Expedition Reserve especially for the St. Charles, Missouri, Lewis and Clark Bicentennial Commemoration in May 2004. The beer is a medium-bodied amber ale. *Bill Yenne*

Some about the Sise of house flies ... the Misquitors [are] So thick & troublesom that it was disagreeable and painfull." The captains used more than a dozen spelling variations for the word *mosquito*.

The Corps of Discovery had seen evidence of Indian camps along the way, but their first face-to-face contact with the indigenous people of the plains did not occur until the end of July. The Corps was still considerably downriver from the main stronghold of the Sioux and traveling through the territory that was home to many smaller plains tribes. These included the Kansa, Missouri, Pawnee, Omaha, and Oto. The tribes are discussed in the journals with a withering variety of misspellings. The Kansa were referred to as Canzan and Canseze, while the Omaha were usually referred to as the "Mahar." The Pawnee were called Pani or Pania.

On July 23, the Corps of Discovery stopped at a place 10 miles above the mouth of the Platte River where Interstate 80 now crosses Interstate 29, slightly south of the metropolitan area that encompasses Omaha, Nebraska, on the west side of the Missouri River and Council Bluffs, Iowa, on the east. The Corps of Discovery called the place Camp White Catfish, after they caught a notable number of these fish there. Today, it is the location of Iowa's Lake Manawa State Park.

Having seen evidence that Oto, Omaha, or other people had been in the area recently, the captains sent George Drouillard and Pierre Cruzatte to look for them and invite them to come to the camp. The men found only an abandoned encampment about 18 miles inland on the western side of the Missouri River.

Five days later, Drouillard and the Corps' hunting party that operated ashore made contact with a lone hunter. He explained that he was of the Missouri tribe, but was hunting with the Oto people. Bearing in mind Jefferson's orders to "Make yourself acquainted" with the Indian nations, Lewis sent the French boatman known as La Liberté to accompany the Missouri man to the main group of Indians and invite them to come to meet the Corps of Discovery.

Lewis and Clark's, an American restaurant and public house, is located on the corner of First Capitol and Main Street in historic St. Charles, Missouri. It was near here that Clark collected Lewis on May 15, 1804, the expedition's second day. The restaurant didn't exist until 1985, but they certainly would have enjoyed dining here. The captains would probably also have liked the restaurant's sister establishment, Trailhead Brewing, which is also located in St. Charles. *Bill Yenne*

The Lewis and Clark Boat House and Nature Center is located on the Missouri River at Bishop's Landing in St. Charles, Missouri. It is an educational facility that features exhibits that describe the Lewis and Clark expedition, the town of St. Charles, and the Missouri River ecosystem. The Boat House is also home to the handmade replica rivercraft that are operated by Discovery Expedition—that is, when the vessels are not on the river. *Bill Yenne*

Ten weeks out of St. Charles, Lewis and Clark had reached another world. It was a land still populated by people who lived as they had long before Europeans had arrived on the continent. It was also a land where most people had never seen a European or an American of European descent. They were nearly 5,000 miles from the Paris salon where pale-skinned men had inked the paper that made them citizens of the United States rather than subjects of the French emperor, and they had no idea that this had happened. They couldn't conceive of such a thing, nor could they have cared less. Lewis, on the other hand, was here to inform them that they had a new father in Washington—yet another place that could not have been farther from their daily concerns.

A modern replica of the Lewis and Clark expedition flagship is underway by oar-power on the Missouri River. Rowing against the current was always a difficult task, but when there was no wind for the sail and pulling or poling was not possible, the Corps manned the oars. *Chad Coppess, South Dakota Department of Tourism*

A replica of the Corps of Discovery flagship makes its way up the Missouri River through Jefferson City. The Missouri State Capitol is in the background. The original flagship passed this point on June 4, 1804. It returned again the following spring, but Lewis and Clark had continued west without it. *Missouri Tourism New Bureau*

The lower Missouri River in springtime appears today much as it may have in 1804 as the Lewis and Clark expedition started out. The brushy bottom land that parallels the river would have made going ashore to pull the boats impossible, but oars, poles, and sails were available for motive power. *Bill Yenne*

Near the shore of the Missouri, the current was less and the water was shallow, so poles were used to propel the expedition's boats. These re-enactors aboard a replica of the white pirogue are dressed as the French boatmen hired by Lewis and Clark. *Chad Coppess, South Dakota Department of Tourism*

THE TRAIL BEGINS   49

Logjams, such as this one in central Missouri, were a recurring hazard for the expedition when their boats were poling nearer the shore of the river. We can see in this image why the Missouri was referred to as "the Big Muddy." *Bill Yenne*

This pencil drawing depicts the Corps of Discovery traveling on the Missouri River as storm conditions set in. The men are attempting to keep the boat from being dashed against the shore by strong winds. *National Park Service, Harpers Ferry Center, artist Richard Schlecht*

The Corps of Discovery Statue at Clark's Point in Case Park, Kansas City, includes Lewis, Clark, and Sacagawea. She did pass through Kansas City but never with Lewis or Clark. She came this way in 1809 with Toussaint Charbonneau on her visit to St. Louis. *Kansas City Convention and Visitors Bureau*

Chapter Three

"The Air is Pure and Healthy, So Far As We Can Judge"

William Clark's sunny description, penned on August 3, 1804, reflected the optimistic mood that was soon tempered by hardship, but which could, for now, be relished. Two days before, as the Corps of Discovery waited for the Oto chiefs to come and meet them, Clark had celebrated. "This being my birth day," he wrote, "I order'd a Saddle of fat Vennison, an Elk fleece & a Bevertail to be cooked and a Desert of Cheries, Plumbs, Raspberries Currents and grapes of a Sup[erio]r. quallity."

This 1955 Dean Cornwell illustration depicts the red-headed William Clark taking a sextant reading from a bluff overlooking the Missouri River on August 3, 1804. This was the day the captains put on their dress uniforms to have their council with the Oto chiefs north of what is now Omaha, Nebraska. *Montana Historical Society, Gift of New York Life Insurance*

This monument atop a bluff a short distance north of Council Bluffs, Iowa, commemorates Lewis and Clark and their August 1804 council with the Oto Chiefs. *Bill Yenne*

Although he observed that "Musquetors [were] verry troublesom," he preferred to think about the "Cool fine eveninge," and muse that "The Praries Contain Cher[ri]es, Apples, Grapes, Currents, Raspburry, Gooseberris Hastlenuts and a great Variety of Plants & flours not Common to the US." By now, the Corps of Discovery had reached the modern highway equivalent of Milepost 535 from Camp Dubois.

The following day, six Oto and Missouri men, accompanied by a French trader, arrived at the camp to meet with Lewis and Clark, who were decked out in their dress uniforms. Because they seemed to be men of prominence, the co-captains described the men as "chiefs." Lewis and Clark informed them that they were glad to see them and arranged a formal meeting, or council. At this council, the co-captains and the chiefs shared pipes of tobacco and exchanged pleasantries and token gifts. As he had been instructed by Jefferson, Lewis made careful note of their language and customs.

High cliffs rose up sharply on the eastern side of the Missouri River south of this point, so Lewis and Clark named the place Council Bluff. They noted that the bluff was "High &

leavel on top well Calculated for a fort to Command the Countrey and river the low bottom above high water & well Situated under the Command of the Hill for Houses to trade with the Natives a butifull Plain both abov and below." Today, these cliffs overlook the city of Council Bluffs, Iowa.

The actual council itself, however, did not take place on these bluffs. It happened across the Missouri River and farther north, near where the U.S. Army constructed Fort Atkinson in 1820. The site is now Fort Atkinson State Historical Park, located in the town of Fort Calhoun, Nebraska. A life-size bronze sculpture called "First Council" depicts the first meeting of Lewis and Clark with officials of an indigenous tribe.

Atop a bluff north of Council Bluffs is an elaborate monument acknowledging Lewis and Clark. This site provides a grand view of the Missouri River valley, of the city of Council Bluffs, and the Omaha metropolitan area. Today, a steep bicycle trail reaches the monument from the Western Historic Trails Center in Council Bluffs. This center, which presents a program entitled "How the West Was Won, Lost, and Transformed," features exhibits related to the Lewis and Clark Trail, as well as the mid-nineteenth century emigrant roads that passed through this area, such as the Oregon, Mormon, and California trails.

Upriver, U.S. Highway 75 parallels the Missouri River north of Omaha, and Interstate 29 follows the river north of Council Bluffs. Access to the river from the latter highway may be had by way of boat ramps at the Wilson Island Recreation Area (Exit 72), the DeSoto

This view looks across the Missouri River from the Lewis and Clark Monument above Council Bluffs, Iowa, on a rainy spring day. The skyline of Omaha, Nebraska, can be seen in the mist in the distance. The actual council took place in Nebraska not on the bluffs. *Bill Yenne*

National Wildlife Refuge (Exit 75), the Little Sioux Access (Exit 95), the Huff-Warner Access (Exit 105), Whiting Access (Exit 120), or Snyder Bend County Park (Exit 134). In this area during the first week of August 1804, Lewis and Clark noted "mosquitors thick and troublesome," and the same experience with these creatures is still possible today.

Another headache encountered by the Corps of Discovery in the section of the Missouri north of Council Bluffs was the presence of numerous sandbars and partially submerged snags. The sandbars caused their keelboat to run aground frequently as the crew maneuvered to dodge the snags that posed an even greater peril to navigation.

On the subject of keelboats, people today come from around the world to indulge their interest in these vessels at this section of the river. Located at Milepost 585, near the town of Onawa, is Iowa's Lewis and Clark State Park. It contains a 250-acre oxbow lake known as Blue Lake. Lewis and Clark reached the lake on or about August 9, 1804, and the lake was probably part of the Missouri River before it changed course during the past two centuries. The man who operates Blue Lake is considered to be the leading authority on the boats of the Lewis and Clark expedition.

Butch "Mr. Keelboat" Bouvier has spent more than two decades researching the boats that Lewis and Clark used in 1804 and building replicas, especially of their flagship. His L&C Replicas is the only company in the United States that

Butch Bouvier became the foremost authority on the watercraft of the Lewis and Clark expedition the hands-on way, by constructing most of the replica vessels that were afloat on the Missouri at the time of the bicentennial. He is seen here aboard the *Best Friend*, a wider variation of the expedition flagship. *Bill Yenne*

The *Discovery*, a replica of the Lewis and Clark flagship built by Butch Bouvier, is seen here on Blue Lake at Iowa's Lewis and Clark State Park. When Lewis and Clark passed this way in August 1804, this section of the lake was probably part of the Missouri River. *Bill Yenne*

specializes in eighteenth- and nineteenth-century human-powered rivercraft. Bouvier's vessels have been used by such filmmakers as Ken Burns, and they appeared in the National Geographic IMAX film about the Lewis and Clark Expedition. Mr. Keelboat and his wife, Catherine, a.k.a. Mrs. Keelboat, recently filmed a History Channel special called *The Technology of the Lewis and Clark Expedition.*

Bouvier has deduced the reasons for Lewis having ordered a standard 55-foot barge design that was narrower than standard.

"Lewis felt that the width of his boat would play a big part in the success or failure of his quest for a water passage to the Pacific," Bouvier explains. "He seemed obsessed with width over other measurements when discussing the river. He only referred to the depth of the water on three or four occasions; he mentioned the length of islands and distance from one point to another often, but he never failed to mention the width of a tributary, channel, etc. I believe he should have been less concerned with width of river and more with depth, as this was the problem he had the most trouble with. I would bet that if he had it to do over, he would take a standard width boat which drew less water."

Bouvier also theorizes that the expedition's keelboat was not a traditional keelboat at all, but rather a barge-type design. In fact, as Bouvier points out, neither Lewis nor Clark ever referred to the vessel as a "keelboat," although Lewis once called it a "keeled boat." For the most part it was "the boat," or as often as not, "the barge." Bouvier points out that the term "barge" generally referred to sheltered harbor and inland water craft. Such flat-bottomed boats cannot handle the large swells in the ocean, but have the shallow draft necessary in rivers.

"It was probably very flat bottomed, built of heavy timbers," Bouvier writes. "Just a barge with an enclosed cabin in the stern. A basic barge design of the era, one of many being built in the Pittsburgh area."

While many marine archaeologists have theories about the details of the vessel that Lewis and Clark used as a flagship, Bouvier's opinion is tempered by the fact that he has actually built and sailed a number of similar vessels. His rivercraft are in service on lakes and rivers throughout the United States, and several are on static display in museums, visitor centers, and state capitols. Bouvier has served as a consultant to the Sioux City Lewis and Clark Visitors Center, the United States Geological Survey's American River traveling display, and the Lewis and Clark Interpretive Center in Hartford. Of the six full-size

Carrying a group of lucky tourists, the keelboat *Discovery* prepares to dock at Lewis and Clark State Park near Onawa, Iowa. *Bill Yenne*

A modern-day river boatman, dressed as an 1804 river boatman, stows gear aboard the *Discovery* at Blue Lake in Iowa's Lewis and Clark State Park. *Bill Yenne*

This side-by-side comparison of two vessels constructed by Butch Bouvier illustrates one of his theories about Meriwether Lewis' choice of boats. On the left, the *Discovery* was built to the dimensions that Lewis specified for the expedition flagship. On the right, the wider *Best Friend* represents what Bouvier believes would have been a better choice in terms of stability. Lewis went with the narrower vessel because of unfounded fears that the expedition would encounter channels too narrow for a wider boat. *Bill Yenne*

This replica cannon aboard the replica *Discovery* is a best guess of how the weapon carried by the real flagship actually looked. Lewis described it only as a "bow pece" and did not elaborate further. Replica pirogues can be seen in the background. *Bill Yenne*

keelboat replicas that were in service as the Lewis and Clark bicentennial began in 2004, Bouvier built five of them.

While Butch Bouvier keeps the memories of the Lewis and Clark watercraft alive, the next major landmark along the Missouri River recalls memories from the first—and only—death to occur among the Corps of Discovery during the expedition. Charles Floyd was a 22-year-old member of "the nine young men from Kentucky" Meriwether Lewis recruited on his way down the Ohio River a year earlier. Lewis considered him a "man of much merit" and promoted him to sergeant.

As early as the end of July 1804, Floyd had been feeling poorly. In a journal entry in which he discussed the aches and pains, ticks and boils being suffered by the men generally, Clark specifically singled out Floyd, observing that he was "verry unwell."

By August 19, as the corps was encamped near a Mahar (Omaha) village just south of today's Sioux City, Iowa, Clark noted that attempts to relieve him were "without Success." As Floyd worsened, the Captains spent most of the day in a council with the Mahars, during which they broke out a few drams of their precious Kentucky whiskey.

Back at camp, Clark wrote that the Corps was much alarmed at Floyd's situation, which the captains diagnosed

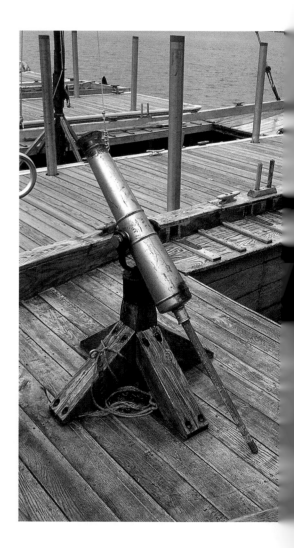

as "Beliose Cholick." Some people translate this as "bilious colic," although Clark may have meant "bellicose colic." In fact, Floyd probably had appendicitis. Nobody really knows. Even in the twenty-first century and in the best of hospitals, this malady goes improperly diagnosed, with fatal results, all too often.

On August 20, as the men were preparing him for a warm bath, Charles Floyd died. A ruptured appendix is a painful way to die, but even if the best doctors of the age could have been brought to his side, there would have been nothing they could have done to save him. Even today, the prognosis is grim.

Clark noted that he died with composure, having said that he was going away. He was buried—with full military honors—atop a high round hill overlooking the Missouri River that they called Floyd's Bluff. A post was erected at his head with his name, rank, and the date. Lewis read the funeral service over him. His death, just three months after they set out from St. Louis, had to have been a wake-up call to the Corps of Discovery that they were in for hard times. In fact, their fears would be unfounded. Floyd would be the only member of the Corps to die during the Lewis and Clark expedition.

This happy fact had to have been obvious on September 4, 1806, when the explorers returned to Floyd's Bluff almost exactly two years later. Both of the captains ascended the hill where they found that the grave had been opened

This roadside sign marks the Lewis and Clark trail in Iowa's Lewis and Clark State Park. In fact, the trail in these parts was on the Missouri River, rather than on land. *Bill Yenne*

Lewis and Clark were fascinated with prairies dogs, which Lewis dubbed "barking squirrels." They spent several hours pouring water down the prairie dog holes to try to drive the specimens out into the open. *National Park Service, Harpers Ferry Center, artist Richard Schlecht*

This view looks south along the Missouri River and Interstate 29 about 676 highway miles from Camp Dubois. It was near the tall, white grain elevator on the horizon that the Corps of Discovery was camped when Sergeant Charles Floyd died of appendicitis on August 20, 1804. The bridge visible near the elevator is the Sergeant Charles Floyd Memorial Bridge. The town on the left is Sergeant Bluff, Iowa. *Bill Yenne*

The imposing Sergeant Floyd Monument was completed in 1901 on a bluff south of Sioux City, Iowa, and commands an excellent view of the Missouri River valley. The 100-foot monument is made of Kettle River sandstone and resembles the Washington Monument. Nine feet square at the base and six feet square at the top, the Egyptian-style obelisk is capped with aluminum connected to copper grounding wires to protect it from lightning. *Bill Yenne*

This is the bronze plaque on the Sergeant Floyd Monument. The huge obelisk marks the final resting place of his mortal remains. *Bill Yenne*

This diorama within the Sioux City Lewis and Clark Interpretive Center depicts the Corps of Discovery assembled for the funeral of Sergeant Floyd. Lewis and Clark are depicted here in their dress uniforms by animatronic mannequins. The uniforms created for the members of the Corps are as accurate as possible, right down to the color of the metal trim on the captains' uniforms. Lewis, as an infantry captain, has silver, while Clark's uniform is trimmed in brass, denoting his commission in the artillery. *George Lindblade, Sioux City Lewis and Clark Interpretive Center*

"by the nativs and left half Covered." As they restored the site, Clark "observed near Sergt Floyds Grave a number of flurishing black walnut trees, these are the first which I have seen decending the river."

During the ensuing half century, the Missouri River gradually eroded Floyd's Bluff. By 1857, this erosion had exposed the end of the sergeant's grave, so the citizens of nearby Sioux City reburied his remains in a walnut coffin, some 600 feet back from the river. In 1895, the second grave was opened and the remains moved again. On August 20 of that year, a slab of engraved marble 4 feet by 8 feet was placed over the grave site.

Four years later, the Floyd Memorial Association was formed in Sioux City to begin work on a 100-foot monument. The project was completed in March 1901. The capstone was laid on April 22, and the monument was formally dedicated on May 30, 1901. Today,

The view is along Interstate 29 and the Missouri with Sioux City, Iowa, in the distance and Dakota City, Nebraska, on the opposite shore. *Bill Yenne*

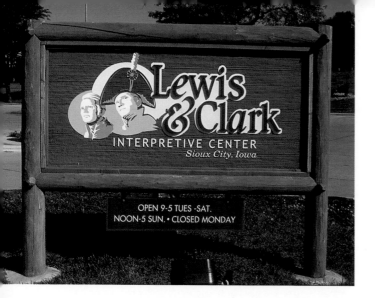

The Sioux City Lewis and Clark Interpretive Center opened in 2004, just in time for the bicentennial. It is located on a site overlooking the Missouri River. The center was built with funds solely from the Missouri River Historical Development, the nonprofit organization that holds the license for riverboat gaming in Woodbury County. *Bill Yenne*

Young scholars on a field trip enjoy the hands-on activities offered by the Sioux City Lewis and Clark Interpretive Center. *George Lindblade, Sioux City Lewis and Clark Interpretive Center*

In front of the Sioux City Lewis and Clark Interpretive Center is a 14-foot bronze sculpture by Colorado artist Pat Kennedy that depicts Lewis, Clark, and Lewis' dog. Kennedy is represented by Boody Fine Arts of St. Louis. *Bill Yenne*

the monument can be seen overlooking Interstate 29 about 2 miles south of the main downtown Sioux City exits. There is no interstate exit for the monument, but it can be reached from Sioux City by backtracking along Lewis Boulevard. Milepost 676 from Camp Dubois is located at the monument.

On the north side of town, near Exit 149 and overlooking the Missouri River, is the Sioux City Lewis and Clark Interpretive Center. It opened in 2004 for the bicentennial of the expedition's pass through this section of the Missouri. The experiences of the Corps of Discovery in this area are the principal focus of the exhibits, and Sergeant Floyd's funeral is the centerpiece. Dozens of interactive devices, including animatronic mannequins, the changing river exhibit, map-making tools, flip books, stamping stations, and brass-rubbing stations underscore the "do touch" philosophy of the center to the delight of patrons, especially kids. Outside, a sculpture by artist Pat Kennedy depicts Lewis, Clark, and Lewis' "dogg of the Newfoundland breed," named Seaman. Kennedy chose to portray the two men in uniform

because they typically donned their dress uniforms for their meetings with Indian leaders as they traveled northward near here in 1804.

If they remember Sergeant Charles Floyd in Sioux City, they remember his successor in Elk Point, South Dakota. The town itself is named for the game that the expedition hunted and dined upon in the area, but this is secondary to the story of Patrick Gass. Less than a mile from the Sioux City Interpretive Center, one crosses the Big Sioux River, enters South Dakota, and marks 683 odometer miles on modern highways from Camp Dubois.

At Milepost 697 is the town of Elk Point, a place that marks the other side of the coin represented by the tragedy of Sergeant Floyd. Following Floyd's death, the captains decided to allow the Corps of Discovery to elect a replacement sergeant from within the group. On August 22, 1804, two days after Sergeant Floyd was laid to rest, Private Gass received 19 votes in what is celebrated as the first election by American citizens west of the Mississippi. In an interesting and ironic twist, Floyd was the first member of the Corps of Discovery to die, and Gass was the last. He passed away in 1870, 66 years later, at the age of 99. One of the older members of the expedition, Gass was 33 when the Corps set out. Historians will recall that Gass' journal, which was published in 1807, was actually the first full account of the expedition to be released and predated the publication of the journals of either Lewis or Clark.

The honor still accorded with Sergeant Floyd and Sergeant Gass, along with the popularity of the Sioux City Interpretive Center, illustrate the way the Lewis and Clark expedition is still remembered and revered in the American Heartland.

Seen here under construction in 2004, the Garden of Discovery exhibit at the Sioux City Lewis and Clark Interpretive Center showcases formal gardens with a two-acre reconstructed prairie as a backdrop. The formally designed sections highlight the plant species encountered and collected by the Lewis and Clark expedition that Meriwether Lewis described as "new to science," such as curlycup gumweed, ten-petal blazing-star, rocky mountain beeplant, and buffaloberry. *Bill Yenne*

A re-enactor portraying Lewis or Clark makes sketches of native plants found along the Missouri River near where it passes from Iowa into South Dakota. *Chad Coppess, South Dakota Department of Tourism*

The Corps of Discovery re-enactors stand at attention. The man in the foreground portrays a civilian and may be the expedition's legendary hunter, George Droulliard. The U.S. Army regulations required the military personnel to be clean-shaven, and in August 1804, the captains still strictly followed the book. *Chad Coppess, South Dakota Department of Tourism*

On August 22, 1804, two days after Sergeant Floyd's funeral, the captains permitted the Corps of Discovery to elect a successor sergeant from among the privates. The first election by American citizens west of the Mississippi took place at what is now Elk Point, South Dakota. The town proudly holds regular re-enactments of the historic event, such as the one seen here. *Chad Coppess, South Dakota Department of Tourism*

Re-enactors portraying Lewis and Clark prepare to count the ballots in the Elk Point, South Dakota, re-enactment of the historic 1804 election of a new sergeant for the Corps. In each re-enactment, the person who portrays Private Patrick Gass wins with 19 votes. *Chad Coppess, South Dakota Department of Tourism*

St. Louis September 23d 1806.

It is with pleasure that I announce to you the safe arrival of myself and party at 12 OClk today at this place with our papers and baggage. In obedience to your orders we have penetrated the Continent of North America to the Pacific Ocean, and sufficiently explored the interior...

...are covered with eternal snows; however a passage over these mountains is practicable from the latter part of June to the last of September, and the cheap rate at which horses are to be obtained from the Indians of the Rocky Mountains and West of them, reduces the expences of transportation over this portage to a mere trifle. The navigation of the Kooskooske, the South East branch of the Columbia...

Chapter Four

Where the Spirits and Buffalo Roam

A curious legend that Lewis and Clark heard from the native people led to the captains' first view of the great bison herds that formed an enduring part of the folklore of the American West through the nineteenth century. The local tribes had convinced the captains that 18-inch tall devils, armed with arrows, inhabited a prairie hill at Milepost 717 from Camp Dubois, near what is now Vermillion, South Dakota.

Where the buffalo still roam. In August 1804, Lewis and Clark started seeing the legendary huge herds of American Bison on the Great Plains. Today, herds of the big animals can be seen grazing, even near lightly traveled secondary roads, across the Dakotas. Although they are now fewer in number, the setting where one sees herds today is virtually unchanged since 1804. *Bill Yenne*

On August 25, 1804, Lewis and Clark "Concluded to go and See the Mound which was viewed with Such [terror] by all the different Nations in this quarter." Accompanied by Sergeant Ordway, Corporal Warfington, George Drouillard and several others, they hiked inland to "the Mound which the Indians Call Mountain of little people or Spirits," finding it "a Conic form . . . in an extensive Valley."

They arrived at noon with the blistering sun directly over their heads. Clark reported that Lewis' dog, Seaman, was "So Heeted & fatigued we was obliged Send him back to the Creek," and added that "Capt Lewis much fatigued from heat the day it being verry hot & he being in a debilitated State. . . and Several of the men complaining of Great thirst."

In observing the hill, now known officially as Spirit Mound, they discussed the possibility of it being an artificial structure that had been constructed by prehistoric people. The Corps of Discovery was familiar with the great Cahokia Mounds, which were close to Camp Dubois where they had spent the previous winter.

"The reagular form of this hill would in Some measure justify a belief that it owed its Orrigin to the hand of man," Clark wrote. "But as the earth and loos pebbles and other Substances of which it was Composed, bare an exact resemblance to the Steep Ground which border on the Creek in its neighbourhood we Concluded it was most probably the production of nature. The only remarkable Charactoristic of this hill admiting it to be a naturial production is that it is insulated or Seperated a considerable distance from any other, which is verry unusial in the naturul order or disposition of the hills."

As an explanation for the "little people or Spirits," Clark postulated that "the wind from whatever quarter it may blow, drives with unusial force over the naked plains and against this hill; the insects of various kinds are thus involuntaryly driven to the mound by the force of the wind, or fly to its Leward Side for Shelter; the Small Birds whoes food they are, Consequently resort in great numbers to this place in Surch of them; Perticularly the Small brown Martin of which we saw a vast number hovering on the Leward Side of the hill, when we approached it in the act of Catching those insects; they were So gentle that they did not quit the place untill we had arrivd. within a fiew feet of them. . . One evidence which the Inds Give for believing this place to be the residence of Some unusial Spirits is that they frequently discover a large assemblage of Birds about this mound is in my opinion a Suffient proof to produce in the Savage mind a Confident belief of all the properties which they ascribe it."

Spirit Mound is located on South Dakota State Route 19, a few miles north of State Route 50. From this point, modern day travelers following the Lewis and Clark Trail won't follow the interstate highway system for a while. With two brief exceptions in Montana, it will be 2,500 miles before an interstate highway again parallels the westbound route of the Corps of Discovery.

The men hiked for four hours in the sweltering heat, and atop the mound, the infamous devils were nowhere to be found. However, the captains did see

Turn right to the Twilight Zone. At Vermillion, South Dakota, one turns on State Route 19 to reach the strange hill that native people thought was inhabited by supernatural gremlins. Lewis and Clark thought it might be the ruins of an ancient pyramid-like structure. *Bill Yenne*

Spirit Mound was privately owned and closed to the public for many years but is now officially administered by the state of South Dakota. The curious may follow the Lewis and Clark trail to its top. *Bill Yenne*

Spirit Mound is a substantial hill when taken in the context of the flatness of the surrounding prairie. When Lewis and Clark struggled to the top on a blistering hot August day in 1804, they came to investigate the reports of the little demons that lived there. They saw nothing supernatural and postulated a scientific explanation. *Bill Yenne*

an incredible sight—a vast ocean of bison. For the remainder of the year, as the Corps of Discovery traveled north across what are now the Dakotas, these great beasts were the primary source of protein for the men.

Present in the tens (or possibly hundreds) of millions at the turn of the nineteenth century, the great American bison—still known almost universally as buffalo—would be virtually extinct by the dawn of the twentieth century. Today, however, there are more than a quarter

This illustration depicts Lewis, Clark, and members of the Corps of Discovery atop Spirit Mound. According to their journals, the men who made it to the top of this hill were more concerned about their thirst than about searching for the "little people or spirits" that were said to inhabit the region. *National Park Service, Harpers Ferry Center, artist Richard Schlecht*

of a million, with the majority in private herds and raised for meat. Across the Dakotas and Montana, it is not unusual to find bison on the menu. Those who enjoy a good steak now and then will almost unanimously choose bison over beef.

The cuisine of the Lewis and Clark Expedition has long been considered only in passing, but it is hard to ignore the culinary side of the daily lives of men who are said to have each eaten as much as nine pounds of meat every day as they pushed their flotilla upstream. Actually, the widely reported nine pounds is disputed by Mary Gunderson, the author of *The Food Journal of Lewis and Clark: Recipes for an Expedition*. She said that the figure is probably closer to six pounds per man, per day.

The Missouri River meanders past Riverside Park in Yankton, South Dakota. This city of 20,000 proudly embraces the fact that the Corps of Discovery camped here. Yankton's Lewis and Clark Festival features re-enactments, Indian cultural activities, and the "bison-tennial" cook-off. *Bill Yenne*

A re-enactor at the Yankton Lewis and Clark Festival patiently explains a collection of replica personal gear to a curious family. *Chad Coppess, South Dakota Department of Tourism*

As a tourist-filled replica of the white pirogue glides past in the background, a re-enactor portraying William Clark gazes thoughtfully toward the festivities unfolding at the Yankton Lewis and Clark Festival. *Chad Coppess, South Dakota Department of Tourism*

A man in a captain's uniform conducts a rope demonstration at a Lewis and Clark re-enactment in South Dakota. Skills with a rope were every bit as important to the men of the Corps of Discovery as they would have been for a nineteenth-century sailor on the high seas. *Kristi Hansen, South Dakota Department of Tourism*

As Lewis and Clark confer between themselves, a group of Sioux wait to exchange token gifts and pleasantries at the Yankton Lewis and Clark Festival. *Chad Coppess, South Dakota Department of Tourism*

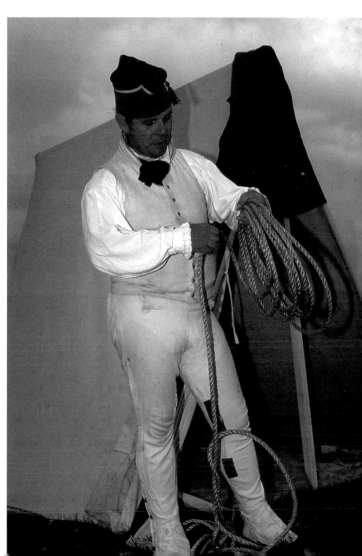

This is the Missouri River upstream from Yankton, South Dakota. The names of the captains are very much in evidence in these parts. Just across the river in Nebraska is the Lewis and Clark State Recreation Area. A few miles farther upstream, Gavin's Point Dam creates Lewis and Clark Lake. *Bill Yenne*

Food writer and culinary historian Mary Gunderson poses with the plaque in Yankton, South Dakota, that identifies the nearby grave of Pierre Dorion, an interpreter that Lewis and Clark hired to help them communicate with the Yankton Sioux. Based in Yankton, Gunderson is the author of *The Food Journal of Lewis and Clark: Recipes for an Expedition*, where she created recipes based on the descriptions in the captains' journals of the meals that the Corps of Discovery ate. *Bill Yenne*

Based in Yankton, South Dakota, just 24 miles upriver from where the captains disembarked on their side trip to Spirit Mound, Gunderson used the captains' own journals to recreate recipes for the meals that the Corps of Discovery probably ate as they crossed the continent—from Mandan and Hidatsa corn and beans to West Coast Salish Indian salmon dishes.

A nationally noted food writer and culinary historian, Gunderson has presented her "paleocuisineology," a fact-filled, but light-hearted approach to food history, at the National Archives in Washington, D.C., at the Lewis and Clark Exposition at Thomas Jefferson's Monticello, and for various humanities councils.

"When I first considered writing about foods of the Lewis and Clark Expedition . . . I wondered if the food tasted good," she says. "While reading the Lewis and Clark journals and letters, I discovered that Meriwether Lewis and William Clark wrote about food almost every day. . . . We know when the explorers ate the last of their butter and when they first tasted buffalo."

Spanning the breadth of the expedition, from the dining rooms of Philadelphia to the prairies near Yankton to the salmon feeds on the Pacific shore, the recipes in *The Food Journal of Lewis and Clark: Recipes for an Expedition* confirm that the food did taste good.

Just a bit upstream from the modern city of Yankton, the Corps of Discovery finally entered the domain of the Sioux. Jefferson instructed Lewis to make a "favorable impression" on the Sioux Nation because of the immense power they wielded on the plains. The tribe's reputation was known far and wide. Of all the Native Tribes encountered by the Corps of Discovery, the Sioux were the most feared by the other Plains tribes—especially the Mandan and Arikara. The captains also approached the Sioux with trepidation.

With Pierre Dorion translating, Lewis and Clark held their council with the Yankton Sioux at Calumet Bluffs, in what is now South Dakota, on August 29, 1804. They met with more than 70 people, including 5 chiefs. The woman in the foreground is not Sacagawea. They would not meet her until the coming winter. *National Park Service, Harpers Ferry Center, artist Richard Schlecht*

To some, the Corn Palace in Mitchell, South Dakota, is the capitol of kitsch, and to others it is a celebration of the signature crop of America's heartland. Each year several panels on the exterior of the Corn Palace are decorated with ears of locally grown corn. A different theme is chosen each year, and murals are designed to reflect that theme. In 2004, the bicentennial of the Lewis and Clark expedition, there was only one choice of theme. The designer was Cherie Ramsdell, an art teacher at Mitchell High School who grew up in Wagner, South Dakota. *Bill Yenne*

Historically the largest tribe on the Great Plains, the Sioux are still the largest tribe in that area today. They were the dominant political, military, and cultural force on the northern plains from before the eighteenth century until the 1870s. They were nomads without fixed settlements whose culture and economy revolved around following the great bison herds across the plains. At its apogee, the Sioux homeland spanned the area from the Rocky Mountains to the Mississippi River, including the southern parts of what are now Montana, the Dakotas, and Minnesota, as well as much of Wyoming, Nebraska, and Iowa.

They were first called "Sioux" by the eighteenth-century French traders, a name that would be almost in universal use for more than 200 years. The term was a truncation of the Chippewa word *Nadouessioux*, which means "little snakes." The Chippewa applied this derogatory nomenclature to all the Plains tribes that shared the Hokan-Siouan language. The Sioux are the principal people of this linguistic group, which also includes Plains tribes such as the Iowa, Oto, Omaha, Ponca, Osage, Kansa, Quapaw, and Winnebago. On the northern plains, the Hidatsa and Mandan—who Lewis and Clark met late in 1804—also spoke a Hokan-Siouan dialect.

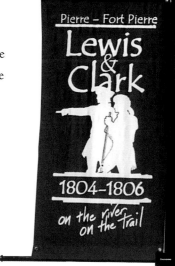

Many jurisdictions along the Lewis and Clark trail created special graphics to celebrate the bicentennial. Pierre and its sister city, Fort Pierre, across the Missouri River, used the silhouette from the national trail sign on their banners. *Bill Yenne*

Pierre, South Dakota, is America's smallest state capital city and one of three state capitals through whose city limits Lewis and Clark are certain to have passed. The other two cities are Jefferson City, Missouri, and Bismarck, North Dakota. They probably missed the city limits of Helena, Montana, but they must have come close. *Bill Yenne*

The Sioux are, in turn, geographically subdivided into three distinct, but closely related, groups. Each speaks a separate but similar Hokan-Siouan dialect. These groups each refer to themselves by a name that means "all Sioux people." From east to west, these three groups refer to all members of the tribe as Dakota, Nakota, and Lakota, respectively. The people themselves never used the term *Sioux* until after the beginning of the reservation era in the late nineteenth century. We use the term in the context of this work because it is the most widely used term in the Dakotas today, and because Lewis and Clark used it—although they misspelled it numerous different ways, usually inserting the letter *e* in various places.

Before meeting the Sioux, the captains had met another legend of the plains, Pierre Dorion. This 64-year-old Cajun trapper, whose name was often misspelled by the captains, had traded and lived with the Sioux for decades, married at least one Sioux woman, and knew their language well. Lewis and Clark had crossed paths with him on June 12 as he made his way north on a trading trip. The captains asked him to serve as their Sioux interpreter.

On August 27, they learned there was a large gathering of the Yankton branch of the Sioux tribe just upstream from what is now Yankton. Accompanied by Nathaniel Pryor and Pierre Cruzatte, Dorion went to their camp to "invite their Great Chiefs to Come and Counsel with" Lewis and Clark. This first summit with the Sioux occurred at Calumet Bluffs on August 29. The captains met with what they counted as 5 chiefs and around 70

On September 24, 1804, William Clark went ashore near the site of present-day Pierre to meet with a Lakota chief named Buffalo Medicine and his entourage and to discuss some allegedly stolen horses. For the next 48 hours, disagreements between the Lakota and the Corps came close to disaster many times before it was diffused. *Chad Coppess, South Dakota Department of Tourism*

This re-enactment finds Corps of Discovery personnel and Lakota warriors aboard a replica of the white pirogue. The people ashore seem oblivious to the fact that this recreates one of the most tense and potentially catastrophic moments of the entire expedition. On September 25, 1804, as several Lakota were being rowed ashore in the pirogue from a meeting aboard the flagship, Clark and Black Buffalo got into a disagreement. During this, an overt effort was made to steal the boat. *Chad Coppess, South Dakota Department of Tourism*

men, plus an unspecified number of women. They gave the Sioux some tobacco and "a few Kittles for them to Cook in" and agreed to meet again the next day. In the course of his notes of the meeting, Clark penned one of the first written descriptions of the plains Indian teepee, calling it "handsom of a Conic form Covered with Buffalow Roabs Painted different Colours and all Compact."

The following day, the captains met again with the Sioux and Dorion translated Lewis' speech. The captains dined with the Sioux leaders and gave them peace medals bearing the likeness of their "new father" (President Jefferson), while the corps impressed them with a demonstration firing of the cannon aboard their flagship.

After the Calumet Bluffs meeting, Dorion and the captains parted company, and the old Cajun was given a bottle of whiskey for his trouble. Two years later, the United States War Department hired him as an Indian agent. He died in 1810.

On the night of September 25, 1804, the Corps of Discovery camped here on this large island in the Missouri River. They named it Bad Humored Island, but today it is called Framboise Island, after the French word for raspberries. It is not so much the Lewis and Clark trail as a campsite, but the exact site has never been located. *Bill Yenne*

The Corps of Discovery had been in contact with the native people for about two months and found them generally hospitable but a bit wary of the large group of strangers.

Having met the Yankton Sioux, the Corps of Discovery began to encounter the powerful Teton Sioux, who are speakers of the western, or Lakota, dialect. During the last week of September, they began passing larger and larger Lakota villages.

On September 24, the Corps approached the location on the Missouri River now occupied by

These islands in the Missouri River about a hundred yards upstream from Framboise Island give an idea of what the island may have looked like from the river as Lewis and Clark took refuge there in September 1804. These are still islands, whereas Framboise Island is now a peninsula. The U.S. Highway 14 bridge in the distance connects Pierre and Fort Pierre. *Bill Yenne*

Pierre (pronounced "Pier"), the present-day capital of South Dakota. Here, they counted some 140 tepees, a sizable Lakota encampment.

That morning, as the captains prepared some Jefferson peace medals to present to the Lakota chiefs, Private John Colter, who had been ashore hunting, returned with some good and bad news. He had shot four elk, but his horse had been stolen by some young Lakota men. Soon after, they saw five Lakota on the river bank who expressed an interest in coming aboard the flagship. Lewis and Clark informed them that they had come as friends and wished to continue as such, but that "Some of their young Men had Stolen a horse Sent by their Great Father [Jefferson] to their great Chief, and we Should not Speak to them any more untill the horse was returned to us again."

Two miles farther on, more Lakota were encountered and Clark went ashore. He smoked a pipe with a chief called Buffalo Medicine, who claimed that he

North of Pierre, the appropriately named, two-lane South Dakota State Route 1804 follows the section of the Missouri River that Lewis and Clark followed in the autumn of 1804. *Bill Yenne*

Roadside businesses, such as this antique emporium in Mobridge, South Dakota, have responded to the needs of people following the Lewis and Clark trail. None of the antiques available date from the passage of the Corps in 1804. *Bill Yenne*

Near Glenham, South Dakota, the Lewis and Clark trail shifts to U.S. Highway 12 and South Dakota State Route 20. The operable word here is *west*. We also see that we are now following the Yellowstone Trail, but Highway 12 will not actually touch that river for another 300 miles. The Lewis and Clark trail will soon leave these roads, but it will reconnect to Highway 12 to cross the Idaho panhandle, much farther to the west. *Bill Yenne*

knew nothing of the horse. Clark apparently decided to drop the issue, noting that "I informed them we would call the grand Chiefs in Council tomorrow."

The following day, Buffalo Medicine, along with Black Buffalo and Partisan (or Partizan), came aboard the flagship to smoke with Lewis and Clark and receive presents. Whiskey was offered, which the chiefs enjoyed, but, as Clark put it, they "Soon began to be troublesom." Black Buffalo let it be known that he "had not recived presents Suffient." As he was rowed ashore in one of the pirogues, Clark attempted to pacify him, but this "had a contrary effect for his insults became So personal and his intentions evident to do me injurey."

Once ashore, an apparent attempt was made to steal the pirogue. Clark drew his sword and Lewis ordered all the men in the boat to prepare to fire. At this, the Lakota warriors on the river bank strung their bows and prepared for a fight. Things could have gotten ugly. The Lewis and Clark expedition was in jeopardy. The cannon aboard the flagship could have done considerable damage and the boats could certainly have escaped, but not without a sizable number of casualties. Because the captains were the center of attention at that moment, they would have been primary targets and one or both would likely have been killed. After a few tense moments, Black Buffalo diffused the situation by ordering the Lakota to stand down and back off.

Rather than camping ashore that night, the Corps of Discovery moved their camp to a nearby island for safety. The captains named their momentary refuge Bad Humored Island. Running parallel to today's city of Pierre, it is now known as Framboise Island after the French word for *raspberries*. Today, it is connected to the mainland by a causeway reached by way of Pierre's South Poplar Avenue. The island is now a popular park area, and the causeway serves as an access for boaters and fishermen wishing to use the Missouri River. This point at the northern end of Framboise Island marks 1,054 highway miles from Camp Dubois.

This is the bridge at Mobridge. The sign tells us that U.S. Highway 12 crosses two bodies of water in one. We are more than 125 highway miles north of Oahe Dam, and the banks of the Missouri are still inundated and distorted beyond how they would have appeared in 1804. Nevertheless, the openness of the surrounding terrain has changed little since the captains came this way. *Bill Yenne*

The U.S. Highway 12 bridge at Mobridge is dwarfed by the scale of the vast, largely unchanged prairie landscape of central South Dakota. It was into these hills where George Drouillard and the other hunters of the Corps of Discovery went to obtain the meat the hard-working boatmen ate during the ascent of the Missouri River. *Bill Yenne*

Traveling north from Pierre, the highway that most closely follows the Missouri is the appropriately designated South Dakota State Route 1804 on the eastern side of the river. Although the highway number evokes the mood of the expedition that made its way through these rolling hills more than two centuries ago, the character of the river has been changed dramatically by the construction of Oahe Dam, five miles north of Pierre, which began in 1948 and ended in 1962. The dam has turned the Missouri from here to beyond the North Dakota border, into Lake Oahe, the fourth-largest manmade reservoir in the United States. The Missouri River name is still used as an alternative to the Lake Oahe designation as one moves north.

While the Oahe Dam has dramatically changed the width of the Missouri and has inundated the shoreline where the Corps of Discovery camped in both 1804 and 1806, it has actually preserved nature in the surrounding countryside by greatly limiting the number of crossing points along the Missouri. There are just two crossing points between Pierre and Bismarck, and commercial development has also been limited. As one drives State Route

1804 today, one is struck by the remarkable remoteness of this road that follows the Lewis and Clark trail.

By crossing the Missouri at Mobridge, which marks 1,193 modern highway miles from Camp Dubois, one may pick up South Dakota State Route 1806 on the western side of the river. This designation commemorates the return trip of Lewis and Clark through South Dakota. Running north to the North Dakota line, it passes through the 2.3 million-acre Standing Rock Indian Reservation, which encompasses land in both states. Standing Rock and the adjacent Cheyenne River Reservation is home to members of the Lakota Sioux and comprise an area roughly equal to Massachusetts and have a population roughly equal to Pierre.

As the Corps of Discovery reached the Mobridge vicinity in early October 1804, they met the Arikara people. Unlike the Sioux, who were primarily nomadic hunters, the Arikara lived in more or less permanent villages and farmed the land. In the economic life of the region, they coexisted with the more powerful Sioux by providing vegetables and tobacco to trade for the meat and hides of the buffalo.

On a linguistic note, Lewis and Clark, like most nineteenth-century travelers who encountered the Arikara, dropped the initial letter in the name and referred to the tribes with variations on the words *Ricara* or *Rickaree*. Many people simply referred to the tribe by *Ree*. These name abbreviations were considered no more derogatory than referring to New Englanders as Yankees or Yanks.

On October 8, at the mouth of the Grand River, near today's Mobridge, the captains went ashore to smoke with the Arikara and present their leaders with Jefferson peace medals. This round of councils was much more cordial than those Lewis and Clark had experienced with the Sioux two weeks before. The Arikara were allied with the Hidatsa and the Mandan, who were also farmers, and lived in the area of the Missouri River in what is now northern North Dakota. As Lewis had discussed with Jefferson before starting out, the plan of the expedition was to go into winter quarters near the Mandan and Hidatsa, who were much more favorably disposed to outsiders than the Sioux.

West of the Missouri River, both Dakotas have designated their river-following roads as State Route 1806 to commemorate the return of the Corps of Discovery in that year. Also straddling both states on the west side is the vast Standing Rock Reservation. In this region, the United States Census Bureau lists more counties with a better-than-two-thirds majority Indian population here than anywhere else. *Bill Yenne*

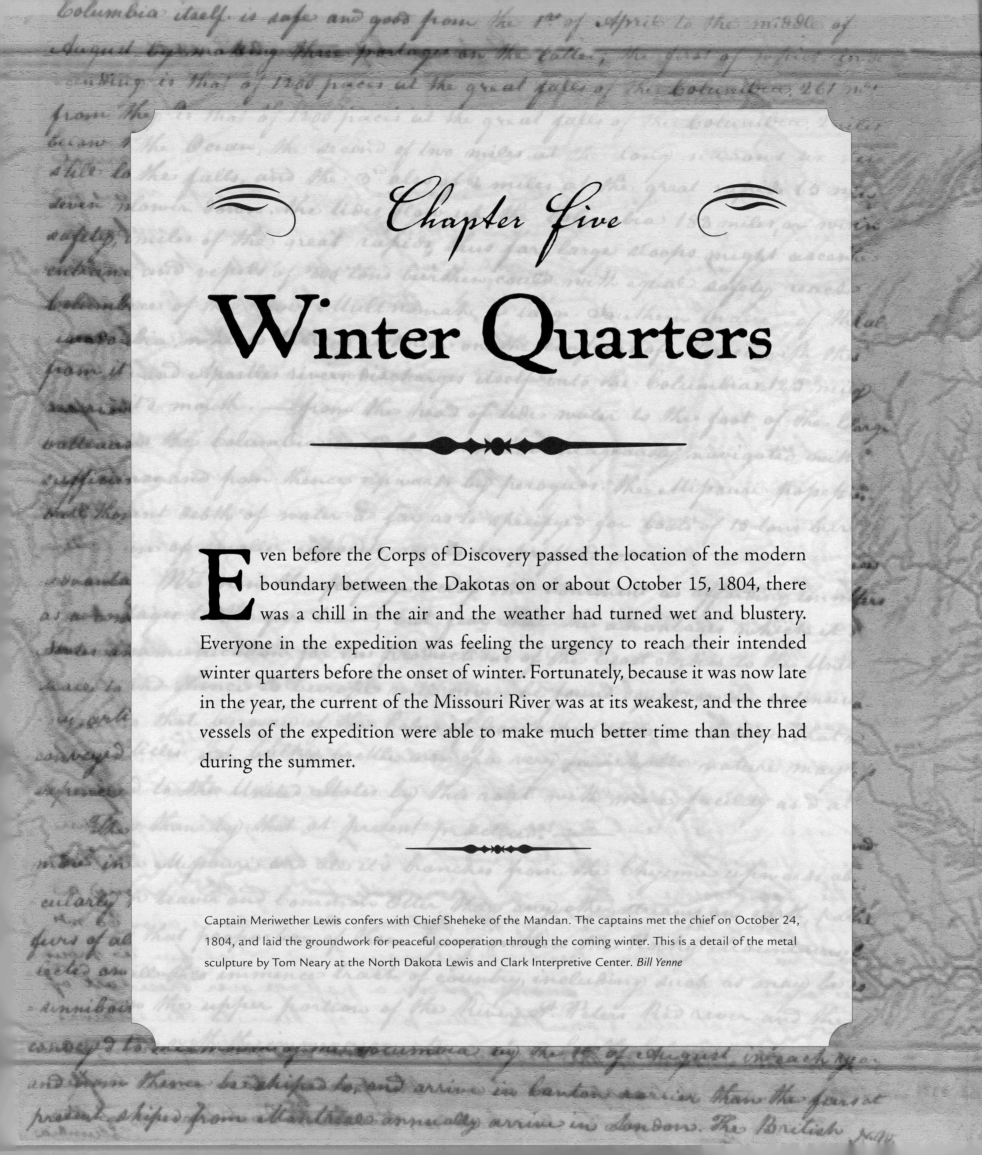

Chapter Five

Winter Quarters

E ven before the Corps of Discovery passed the location of the modern boundary between the Dakotas on or about October 15, 1804, there was a chill in the air and the weather had turned wet and blustery. Everyone in the expedition was feeling the urgency to reach their intended winter quarters before the onset of winter. Fortunately, because it was now late in the year, the current of the Missouri River was at its weakest, and the three vessels of the expedition were able to make much better time than they had during the summer.

Captain Meriwether Lewis confers with Chief Sheheke of the Mandan. The captains met the chief on October 24, 1804, and laid the groundwork for peaceful cooperation through the coming winter. This is a detail of the metal sculpture by Tom Neary at the North Dakota Lewis and Clark Interpretive Center. *Bill Yenne*

North of Bismarck, North Dakota, State Route 1804 closely parallels the Missouri River. In this area, the character of the river is generally as it was in 1804. *Bill Yenne*

North Dakota uses the profile of an American Indian in headdress as a graphic device on its state highway signage. Through the town of Washburn, State Route 1804 and the Lewis and Clark trail coincide with U.S. Highway 83. *Bill Yenne*

On October 21, the journals mention snow for the first time, but it was just a light dusting during the night. By now, they had reached the vicinity of what is now Bismarck, North Dakota, which marks Milepost 1,376 on the modern highway route from Camp Dubois. Also of note for modern travelers is that South Dakota State Routes 1804 and 1806 become North Dakota State Routes 1804 and 1806 as one follows the Missouri River north.

Three days after seeing snow, the Corps met its first Mandan party. They were led by Chief Sheheke, or Big White, who was so named because of his light complexion. In fact, all of the Mandan had light complexions, which did not surprise Lewis and Clark. It only confirmed what they anticipated. As Jefferson had discussed with Lewis, and Lewis passed along to Clark, popular legend held that the Mandan were actually descendants of an expedition led by Prince Madoc, a landless Welsh nobleman who had made one or more voyages from Wales to the Mississippi River late in the twelfth century. Legends repeated on both sides of the Atlantic for several hundred years was that Madoc and his people had settled in the upper reaches of the Missouri. During the eighteenth century, explorers and ethnographers took it for granted that the Welsh and the Mandan were one and the same.

The Corps of Discovery received a warm welcome from the Mandan and their allies, the Hidatsa, who lived in a series of villages located where the Knife River flows into the Missouri River, about 50 miles upriver from where Bismarck now stands. There were several thousand people living at the mouth of the Knife River, more than lived in St. Louis at the time.

Lewis and Clark visited this settlement and camped there and were warmly received by Sheheke and the other leaders of the Mandan and Hidatsa. The Indians gave them a gift of 11 bushels of corn. On November 2, they set out to find a place nearby, but on the opposite shore of the Missouri, to construct the fortified camp where they would spend the winter. They chose a place that Clark described as being "three miles downriver and well supplied with wood." They immediately set about to build what Lewis referred to as the "fortification," which was named "Fort Mandan in honour of our Neighbours."

It had been planned that about a dozen members of the expedition would return to St. Louis aboard the flagship and take the specimens

This aerial photograph provides an excellent overview of the fan-shaped Fort Mandan replica. Built in 1971 by the McLean County Historical Society, it is now managed by the Lewis and Clark Fort Mandan Foundation. Each of the three forts built along the trail by the Corps of Discovery had a distinctive shape that was dictated by what they perceived as their needs at the time. The sloped roof surfaces served to channel and collect rainwater. This configuration was also more defensible. *Lewis and Clark Fort Mandan Foundation*

While most states along the Lewis and Clark trail use a more traditional graphic image in their signage, such as that used on the national Lewis and Clark trail sign, North Dakota has developed a colorful and highly stylized depiction. Between the two captains is Sacagawea, whose name is officially spelled as Sakakawea in North Dakota. *Bill Yenne*

of flora and fauna collected to date, along with the journals and other notes. This contingent, under the command of Corporal Richard Warfington, included the civilian engagés, or boatmen, as well as several soldiers whose infractions to the rules had caused the captains to consider them a liability to the "permanent" Corps of Discovery as it proceeded west in the spring of 1805. The idea was to send the flagship back as soon as the expedition reached winter quarters, but it was already winter with snow on the ground and ice in the river, so they decided to wait until spring.

The severity of the winter at Fort Mandan, which is routine for people living on the northern Great Plains today, stunned the Corps. Nearly every page of their journals for the next several months contains references to snow and cold. Fortunately for posterity, Lewis

This corner of the Fort Mandan replica depicts the quarters that were shared by Lewis and Clark. Buffalo robes provided warmth on those cold winter nights when the temperature stayed well below zero. Weapons were not far away—swords hang on the wall on top of the dress uniform jacket, and a bow and quiver hang on one of the pegs that held the rifle. There is also a pistol on the table. *Bill Yenne*

Inside the parade ground at the Fort Mandan replica, a 15-star American flag flies overhead. The men's quarters were the rooms with fireplaces, and the other enclosed areas were storerooms. *Bill Yenne*

Personal gear carried by each man included the omnipresent hatchet, or tomahawk, a powder horn, and a bag to carry everything from musket balls to the day's field rations. *Bill Yenne*

In another corner of the captains' quarters was the table where they would write in their journals. A map they drew of the nearby section of the Missouri River is visible, along with the all-important sextant. The hatchet was an essential tool that had many uses. *Bill Yenne*

and Clark included thermometers among their scientific gear. They seemed to take a perverse delight in recording the cold that they were experiencing. Among the highlights were 38 degrees below zero on December 12, and five days later it was 43 degrees below. On January 10 it was 40 degrees below, and a month later it was still 16 below zero. On top of the cold was the wind, snow, and ice, which was also described in lurid detail.

The Corps spent the winter hunting and making preparations for the spring voyages, while Lewis and Clark worked on their scientific notes, carefully describing what they had seen so far in terms of flora, fauna, geography, and the native people. The native people from the Knife River Villages were frequent visitors to Fort Mandan, and Lewis and Clark occasionally made return visits. Occasional Assinniboin people, members of the tribe that lived yet farther north in what is now Saskatchewan, also visited the fort. French and English trappers working for the North West Company or Hudson's Bay Company also crossed paths with the Corps during the winter.

On November 4, the captains were called upon by a French trapper named Toussaint Charbonneau, whose name was spelled a myriad of ways—from Charbonie to Sharbono—in their journals. A man in his late thirties, Charbonneau had been working in the back country of Canada and the Upper Missouri for more than a decade. He was a fluent speaker of numerous native languages, including Hidatsa, which Lewis and Clark found especially difficult. For this reason, they hired him as an interpreter and a permanent member of the expedition.

Charbonneau accompanied the Corps the following year, all the way to the Pacific, and back to the Knife River. As an interpreter, he was useful; and as a cook, he was extraordinary. However, in nearly every other skill, he turned out to be a nearly worthless bumbler. His most important contribution to the expedition was the teenager named Sacagawea who had recently become his wife.

Sacagawea was a girl of about 16 who was a member of the Shoshone tribe. She had been captured by the Hidatsa in her native southwestern Montana about four years earlier and taken to the Knife River. It was here that she became one of Charbonneau's two wives. By the time Lewis and Clark met her, Sacagawea was six months pregnant. Clark was present at the birth of their son in the early morning hours of February 11, 1805, and may have aided in the delivery. The boy was named Jean Baptiste, but Clark nicknamed him "Pompey" and called him "Pomp." The captain later took the boy under his wing and looked after his formal education in St. Louis.

In addition to the services of her husband, Lewis and Clark envisioned an important role as a translator that could be played by Sacagawea, and they decided to take her with them. The plan was this: The Shoshone, Sacagawea's people, lived on the eastern slopes of the Rocky Mountains, and they had horses. By the time that the Corps of Discovery reached the eastern slopes of the Rocky Mountains, they would need horses in order to make the crossing. By taking a Shoshone-speaking translator along with them, they would have someone to help them make this important transaction.

As with the Corps of Discovery winter quarters at Camp Dubois, the exact location of Fort Mandan is unknown, and it may very well be under the shifting waters of the Missouri

WHAT'S HER NAME?

Sacagawea's name in Hidatsa means *Bird Woman*, and the correct pronunciation of the Hidatsa word for Bird Woman is "Suh-KAH-guh-we-a," with an emphasis on the second syllable. When Lewis and Clark made contact with her in the early nineteenth century, Hidatsa had no written form, so an English phonetic spelling had to be created, which was done by Nicholas Biddle, who edited the first edition of their journals, which was published in 1814. Although Lewis and Clark themselves spelled her name using a *G*, Biddle substituted a *J* and spelled her name as *Sacajawea*. For more than a century, this spelling became the standardized version that was used in print and in the numerous place names that honored her.

Through the years, both the letter *J* and an unexplained shift to an emphasis on the first syllable led to the mispronunciation "SACK-a-ja-we-a" becoming the common usage. For many years before the Lewis and Clark bicentennial commemoration began, scholars, historians, authors, linguists, and Hidatsa speakers worked to institutionalize the correct pronunciation.

Today, the nationally accepted spelling of her name is *Sacagawea*, pronounced as "Suh-KAH-guh-we-a." This version, which is the correct Hidatsa word for Bird Woman, is what is used in this book.

This 12-foot bronze statue of Sacagawea and her son, Jean Baptiste, was created by Chicago artist Leonard Crunelle and was dedicated on October 13, 1910. Located on the grounds of the North Dakota State Capitol in Bismarck, it depicts a woman somewhat older than Sacagawea was when she traveled west with Lewis and Clark. She is generally believed to have been about 16 in 1804. *Bill Yenne*

The Corps of Discovery's specialized equipment at Fort Mandan would have included traps. Animals such as the beaver were prized for their pelts, but the beaver tail was also a culinary delicacy. *Bill Yenne*

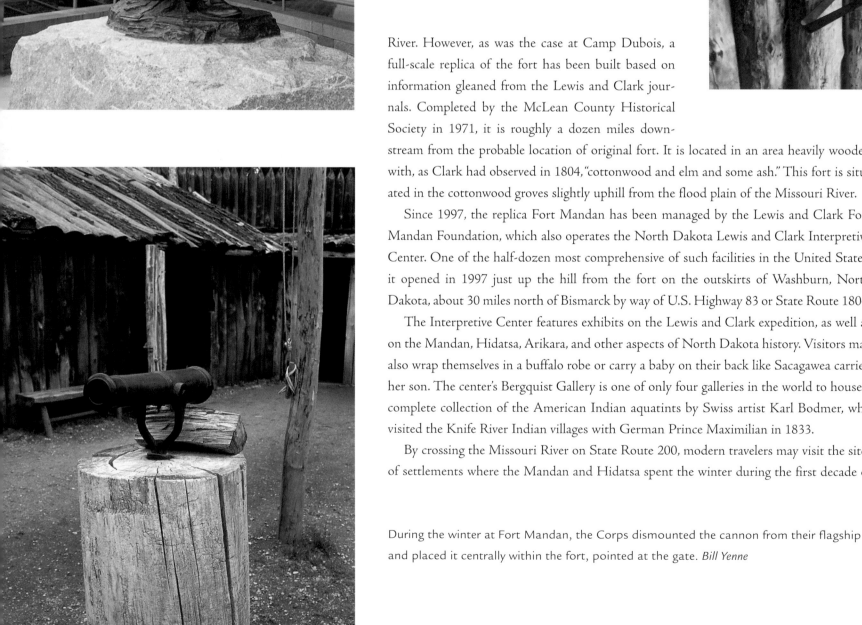

River. However, as was the case at Camp Dubois, a full-scale replica of the fort has been built based on information gleaned from the Lewis and Clark journals. Completed by the McLean County Historical Society in 1971, it is roughly a dozen miles downstream from the probable location of original fort. It is located in an area heavily wooded with, as Clark had observed in 1804, "cottonwood and elm and some ash." This fort is situated in the cottonwood groves slightly uphill from the flood plain of the Missouri River.

Since 1997, the replica Fort Mandan has been managed by the Lewis and Clark Fort Mandan Foundation, which also operates the North Dakota Lewis and Clark Interpretive Center. One of the half-dozen most comprehensive of such facilities in the United States, it opened in 1997 just up the hill from the fort on the outskirts of Washburn, North Dakota, about 30 miles north of Bismarck by way of U.S. Highway 83 or State Route 1804.

The Interpretive Center features exhibits on the Lewis and Clark expedition, as well as on the Mandan, Hidatsa, Arikara, and other aspects of North Dakota history. Visitors may also wrap themselves in a buffalo robe or carry a baby on their back like Sacagawea carried her son. The center's Bergquist Gallery is one of only four galleries in the world to house a complete collection of the American Indian aquatints by Swiss artist Karl Bodmer, who visited the Knife River Indian villages with German Prince Maximilian in 1833.

By crossing the Missouri River on State Route 200, modern travelers may visit the sites of settlements where the Mandan and Hidatsa spent the winter during the first decade of

During the winter at Fort Mandan, the Corps dismounted the cannon from their flagship and placed it centrally within the fort, pointed at the gate. *Bill Yenne*

This view of the Missouri River shoreline shows the effects of several years of high water erosion on the river bank near Fort Mandan. The course of the Missouri is constantly shifting as sections of the banks are worn away and sandbars form in previously open channels. For this reason, it is essentially impossible to pinpoint the exact site of the original Fort Mandan. *Bill Yenne*

This young American Indian woman recently photographed at Fort Mandan is clearly younger than the woman portrayed in the Crunelle bronze. She also appears a bit more carefree than we might have expected of a young woman embarking on a cross-country trip in a dugout canoe with a two-month-old baby. *Lewis and Clark Fort Mandan Foundation*

The North Dakota Lewis and Clark Interpretive Center, located in Washburn, is operated by the Lewis and Clark Fort Mandan Foundation and was opened in 1997. It features exhibits related to the Lewis and Clark expedition at nearby Fort Mandan, as well as exhibits about the fur trade, riverboat era, and the pioneer settlement period in North Dakota. *Bill Yenne*

the nineteenth century. Archaeologists believe that the Hidatsa probably wintered in this location for as long as 500 years. For nearly a thousand years, the region had been a trading hub for the Hidatsa and related peoples, with the primary commodity being Knife River flint. More than 50 archaeological sites suggest that human habitation here may have spanned 8,000 years and ended in 1837, when a smallpox epidemic scourged the area.

Since 1974, this area, north of the little town of Stanton, has been preserved by the National Park Service within the 1,760-acre the Knife River Indian Villages National Historic Site. The earth lodges that existed here two centuries ago—and many centuries before that—are long gone, but numerous circular depressions at three village sites still exist to mark the exact location of each earth lodge. These range from about a dozen feet in diameter up to 40 feet. The middle of the three villages, called Awaxwi, is thought to be the village where Sacagawea was living when she met the captains.

As the billboards and promotional materials for the Fort Mandan Interpretive Center state, "Lewis and Clark Slept Here—146 Times." After the 146th night, it was time to move on. The flagship was sent back down the Missouri River with their samples, notes, and Lewis' letter to Jefferson. On April 7, 1805, Lewis wrote, "Having on this day at 4 P.M. completed every arrangement necessary for our departure, we dismissed the barge and crew with orders to return without loss of time to S. Louis."

The remainder of the Corps of Discovery used the two pirogues and a half dozen dugout canoes to push on into the unknown. Traders and trappers had visited the Knife River Villages, but few Europeans had any notion of what lay to the west. "We were now about to penetrate a country at least two thousand miles in width, on which the foot of civilized man had never trodden; the good or evil it had in store for us was for experiment yet to determine," mused Lewis. "And these little vessels contained every article by which we were to expect to subsist or defend ourselves."

The statue "Mandan Winter" by Washburn sculptor Tom Neary was dedicated at the Interpretive Center during a ceremony attended by the author of this book on June 27, 2004. It includes 12-foot likenesses of Meriwether Lewis, William Clark, and Chief Sheheke. *Bill Yenne*

The Corps now included Toussaint Charbonneau, Sacagawea, and Jean Baptiste. While Charbonneau disappointed the captains greatly, little Pomp delighted them, and his teenage mother turned out to be one of the most important members of the expedition. At one point, not long after they started out from Fort Mandan, one of the pirogues nearly capsized and Charbonneau panicked. Sacagawea, meanwhile, kept her cool and was instrumental in saving several valuable parcels, including the captains' notebooks, from being lost overboard.

To the north of the Knife River Villages on State Route 200 is the massive Garrison Dam. It is the fifth largest earthen dam in the United States and was constructed on the Missouri between 1947 and 1954 by the U.S. Army Corps of Engineers. The dam created Lake Sakakawea, the third-largest manmade reservoir in the country. Only Lake Oahe and Fort Peck Reservoir, also on the upper Missouri, are larger. The name is spelled using the spelling variation of the word *Sacagawea* that is officially used in the state of North Dakota. The impact of the lake that bears her name has obscured the shoreline where she camped with Lewis and Clark as they made their way across what is now northwestern North Dakota in the spring of 1805 and summer of 1806.

The Knife River flows into the Missouri from the west, opposite the sites of both the original and replica Fort Mandans. As with so many areas along the Lewis and Clark route, this area is essentially unchanged with the passage of two centuries. *Bill Yenne*

The visitor center at the Knife River Indian Villages National Historic Site is designed to resemble a traditional Mandan or Hidatsa earth lodge.
Bill Yenne

It is here that the course of the Missouri River, which turns generally north at Kansas City, turns again toward the west. From this point, only State Route 1804 will come close to running parallel to the course of the river, which is now smothered by Lake Sakakawea. At Williston, the lake officially ends. Upstream, the Missouri is once again the Missouri.

Just more than 20 miles west of Williston on State Route 1804—but nearly twice that on the meandering Missouri—one reaches another of the great geographic landmarks of America's great inland river system. It is here that the Yellowstone, a river nearly equal in size to the Missouri, flows into it from the south. With its headwaters in the national park that has shared its name since 1872, the Yellowstone River served as an important trade route later in the nineteenth century during America's westward expansion. In his journals, Clark used the French variation of the name *Roche Jaune*, but he didn't use a consistent spelling of this translation.

To take advantage of the prime trading location where these two main rivers meet, John Jacob Astor's American Fur Company established its Fort Union Trading Post at the strategic confluence of the two rivers in 1828. The hugely lucrative business traded everything from buffalo hides to beaver pelts.

This replica of the type of earth lodges used by the Mandan and Hidatsa was constructed at the Knife River Indian Villages National Historic Site using authentic methods and materials.
Bill Yenne

Inside the replica earth lodge at the Knife River Historic Site is a display of traditional tools, ceremonial objects, and a drum similar to a Celtic bodhran. Paintings on buffalo hides were not decorative, but it was the traditional way the people of the Great Plains recorded their history for posterity. *Bill Yenne*

On April 25, 1805, Lewis wrote that he "ascended the hills from whence I had a most pleasing view of the country, perticularly of the wide and fertile values formed by the missouri and the yellowstone rivers, which occasionally unmasked by the wood on their borders, disclose their meanderings for many miles in their passage through these delightfull tracts of country."

The following day, Lewis dispatched Joseph Fields up the Yellowstone "with orders to examine it as far as he could conveniently and return the same evening."

The captains decided that the Yellowstone was so important that they would split up during their return trip the following year so Clark could explore it. While camped at the confluence, Lewis noted that the Corps "met with two large herds of buffaloe," and Clark observed, "Emence numbers of antelopes in the forks of the river, Buffalow & Elk & Deer . . . also plenty beaver [whose tail was a delicious delicacy] is in every bend."

That night, they dined well.

The many circular depressions in the ground at the Knife River village of Awaxwi each represent the base of a Hidatsa earth lodge that existed in 1805. Awaxwi is the village where Sacagawea lived at that time. *Bill Yenne*

In the 1908 Charles Marion Russell watercolor entitled *York*, the artist takes us inside a Mandan earth lodge in March 1805. Many of the Indian people whom the Corps of Discovery encountered on the upper Missouri River had seen white people, but none had ever seen a black man. They were invariably curious about York, Clark's servant. Clark noted that the one-eyed Hidatsa chief known as Le Borgne was especially inquisitive. He rubbed York's skin in order to wash off the black paint, and only then was he persuaded that York was not a painted white man. *Montana Historical Society, John Reddy*

This is the memo that Captain Meriwether Lewis wrote to President Thomas Jefferson on April 7, 1805, when he was preparing to send the expedition flagship back to St. Louis from Fort Mandan with the notes and specimens collected thus far. He also enclosed an invoice for expenses. *Library of Congress*

This grove along the banks of the Missouri River near the Fort Mandan replica is exactly like the one Lewis and Clark walked through in the spring of 1805 to select long, straight cottonwood trunks to make dugout canoes. *Bill Yenne*

New pioneers over the old terrain. This is the confluence of the Yellowstone and the Missouri rivers as imaged by the Space Shuttle Orbiter *Endeavour* in April 1994. The Missouri enters from the left and the Yellowstone from the bottom. The wide part on the right shows how much of the old river canyon has been filled by Lake Sakakawea, which has been backed up by Garrison Dam since 1947. *NASA*

It is with pleasure that I announce to you the safe arrival
of myself and party at 12 Oclock today at this place with our papers and
baggage. In obedience to your orders we have penetrated the Conte

are covered with eternal snows; however a passage over these mountains is practicable from the latter part of June to the last of
September, and the cheap rate at which horses are to be obtained
from the Indians of the Rocky Mountains and West of them, reduces
the expence of transportation over this portage to a mere trifle.
The navigation of the Kooskooske, the South East branch of the

Chapter Six

Westward Toward the Great Falls

A t Milepost 1,728 from Camp Dubois, a mile past Fort Union National Historic Site, North Dakota State Route 1804 concludes with a sign on the Montana state line stating that the "Pavement Ends." We step back into time on an unnumbered road that follows the Missouri River into the Far West.

In his 1896 oil entitled *Indians Discovering Lewis and Clark*, Montana's legendary Charles Marion Russell takes us back to May 1805. Meriwether Lewis noted in his journal that the Corps passed the remains of fires of 126 Indian lodges that appeared very recent. The Corps saw no one in Montana for nearly three months, but Russell believed people watched them all along their journey. *Montana Historical Society, John Reddy*

Montana, where the state capital is also the county seat of a county named for Lewis and Clark, is extremely integral to their legend. North Dakota and Oregon can both claim many weeks of elapsed time spent within their states, but in both cases, the Corps of Discovery was camped in winter quarters. Montana, on the other hand, can claim more miles of Lewis and Clark trail than any other state. In the other states, the Corps followed more or less the same route coming as going. In Montana, they sought to explore different routes on the return trip, and the two captains split up, so there are actually three Lewis and Clark trails.

Coincidently, much of the Montana landscape that Lewis and Clark saw here—from solitary sandstone-walled river canyons to mountain meadows—remains unchanged since they passed this way.

As one enters the state today—especially from the east—the official state slogan, "Big Sky Country," is certainly an apt description. However, most old-timers recall that this appellation (which is based on the title of A. B. Guthrie's 1947 novel) has only been in use since the early 1960s. Before that, the state's license plates proudly identified Montana as the "Treasure State" because of the riches that spilled forth from the mines at Butte. Since the 1960s, however, people would rather marvel at the vastness of the sky and landscape than the tons of copper ore that once made Butte the "Richest Hill on Earth."

In early May 1805, the Corps of Discovery passed the mouth of the river known to the Hidatsa as "The River Which Scolds at All Others." Rather than adopting this extraordinarily poetic appellation, Lewis noted that it looked milky and designated it as the Milk River, a name it retains to this day. *Bill Yenne*

For the Corps of Discovery, the riches were not in the ground but atop it in the form of the numberless wildlife that could be seen on the rolling hills that surround the Missouri River. Lewis observed, "Game is still very abundant we can scarcely cast our eyes in any direction without percieving deer Elk Buffaloe or Antelopes.

"The country in every derection around us was one vast plain in which innumerable herds of Buffalow were seen attended by their shepperds the wolves," he wrote later on the Montana plains. "The solatary antelope which now had their young were distributed over it's face; some herds of Elk were also seen."

Today, the pronghorn antelope and deer are still present and are legal game in hunting season, but the buffalo are concentrated on ranges and preserves, and the elk have abandoned the plains to take up residence in the mountains farther west.

The civic boosters of Wolf Point on U.S. Highway 2, Montana's "Highline," ask a rhetorical question that invites the traveler to recreate an aspect of the Lewis and Clark experience from the first week of May 1804. *Bill Yenne*

Another denizen of the plains in Lewis and Clark's time that is now found only in the Rockies is the grizzly bear. The captains called it the white,

yellow, or brown bear, which they clearly identified as being a much different animal than the smaller black bear they had been familiar with in the East. The most powerful land mammal in North America then, as now, the grizzly can weigh as much as half a ton and can outrun a horse. "The men as well as ourselves are anxious to meet with some of these bear," wrote Lewis. "The Indians give a very formidable account of the strength and ferocity of this anamal, which they never dare to attack but in parties of six eight or ten persons; and are even then frequently defeated with the loss of one or more of their party. . . . This anamall is said more frequently to attack a man on meeting with him, than to flee from him."

On April 29, 1805, near present-day Culbertson, Montana, Meriwether Lewis had his legendary first encounter with the grizzly. Comparing it to the black bear, he called it "A much more furious and formidable anamal, and will frequently pursue the hunter when wounded. it is asstonishing to see the wounds they will bear before they can be put to death. the Indians may well fear this anamal equiped as they generally are with their bows and arrows . . . but in the hands of skillfull riflemen they are by no means as formidable."

Lewis was lucky. He had killed a 300-pound yearling. With a thick skull analogous to a modern Kevlar helmet, an adult grizzly can be almost indestructible, especially when one considers the firepower carried by the Corps of Discovery.

In the spring of 1805, however, it was the Corps who dined on bear and not vice versa. Later travelers would not be so lucky, and Lewis' own next encounter with a grizzly would not go nearly so smoothly.

The Corps also dined on other things that they could not have earlier imagined. The young Sacagawea introduced them to a wide variety of edible plants that were not then known to the Eastern men of science who had briefed Lewis two years before. The new delicacies ranged from wild licorice to breadroot, which Clark called "white apple" in his journal entry for May 8.

The reservoir on the Missouri River that lies behind Montana's Fort Peck Dam is a vast inland sea and one of the largest reservoirs in the world.
Bill Yenne

This view of U.S. Highway 199, south of Malta, clearly illustrates how wide open the spaces of eastern Montana still are, even after the passage of two centuries. *Bill Yenne*

She had also acquainted the captains with wild onions, which Lewis sensually described as being "white crisp and well flavored."

It was also on May 8 that Clark briefly explored a large northern tributary to the Missouri. In his journal, Lewis observed that this "river possesses a peculiar whiteness, being about the colour of a cup of tea with the admixture of a tablespoonfull of milk. from the colour of it's water we called it Milk River." He then added that the Hidatsa had given the same river the much more colorful designation of "the river which scoalds at all others." Today, this incredibly serpentine river paralleling U.S. Highway 2 for nearly 200 highway miles carries Lewis' name.

Upstream from the confluence of the Milk and Missouri, is the third and largest of the "Big Three" Missouri River dams. Completed in 1940, Fort Peck Dam backs up a reservoir that covers a quarter-million acres where Lewis and Clark camped and hunted in 1805.

While U.S. Highway 2, the so-called "Highline," follows the Milk River across Montana's remote northern tier, no paved road comes within 20 miles of running parallel to the Missouri for the nearly 300 highway miles between Nashua and Loma. For most of this distance, paved roads are more on the order of 50 miles from the Missouri. One exception is U.S. Highway 191, which crosses the Missouri at the remote Fred Robinson Bridge but does not run parallel to it.

For 150 miles upstream from the Fred Robinson crossing, the river runs through what was designated in 2001 as the Missouri Breaks National Monument. The monument's 377,346 acres are managed by the Bureau of Land Management and are in parcels that are intermingled with state of Montana lands and private property. Virtually the only roads in this

In eastern Montana, the Missouri River runs for nearly 300 miles without a parallel paved road within 50 miles. Here, modern explorers may camp with the same sense of wilderness that Lewis and Clark experienced in 1805. *Bill Yenne*

This thicket along the banks of the Missouri River in eastern Montana appears exactly as it might have to Lewis or Clark as they stepped from their pirogue two centuries ago. The only sounds are the river and the wind rustling in the aspen trees. *Bill Yenne*

spectacular wilderness landscape are unpaved. The river runs through it with an official Department of Interior designation as a "Wild and Scenic River." This is an understatement. It is here, if one has the time and watercraft, that it is still possible to experience the sights and sounds—or the absence of sounds—that the Corps of Discovery experienced in 1805.

As Lewis put it, "The hills and river Clifts which we passed today exhibit a most romantic appearance. The bluffs of the river rise to the hight of from 2[00] to 300 feet and in most places nearly perpendicular; they are formed of remarkable white sandstone which is sufficiently soft to give way readily to the impression of water."

May 26 marked another of the great moments in the geographic facet of the expedition. "I beheld the Rocky Mountains for the first time," Lewis noted at a point just west of the Fred Robinson Bridge. "While I viewed these mountains I felt a secret pleasure in finding myself so near the head of the heretofore conceived boundless Missouri; but when I reflected on the difficulties which this snowey barrier would most probably throw in my way to the Pacific, and the sufferings and hardships of myself and party in them, it in some measure

A modern camper pauses to reflect on the dramatic landscape, just as the Corps of Discovery did in 1805. The only way to reach deep inside of the Missouri Breaks National Monument, other than hiking overland, is the way that Lewis and Clark did it—by water on the Missouri River. *Donnie Sexton, Travel Montana*

On June 3, 1805, Lewis and Clark were presented with a conundrum. They reached a point where two rivers of equal size came together. Which one was the Missouri? In his 1988 oil entitled *Decision*, Robert F. Morgan depicts the captains trying to figure out which way to go. They decided to continue south, and Lewis named the other river "Maria's," for his cousin, Maria Wood. *Montana Historical Society, John Reddy*

counterballanced the joy I had felt in the first moments in which I gazed on them; but as I have always held it a crime to anticipate evils I will believe it a good comfortable road untill I am compelled to believe differently." This was a good idea. He would have plenty of time, four months later, to dwell upon sufferings and hardships.

On June 3, near the present town of Loma, Montana, on U.S. Highway 87, the Corps reached the junction of two rivers and had another of the great "what-if" moments of the expedition. As Lewis wrote, "An interesting question was now to be determined; which of these rivers was the Missouri. . . . To mistake the stream at this period of the season, two months of the traveling season having now elapsed, and to ascend such stream to the rocky Mountain or perhaps much further before we could inform ourselves whether it did

Decision Point, the confluence of the Maria's River and the Missouri River. This high-elevation view of the two rivers as they join provides a good look at the situation Lewis and Clark faced during early June in 1805. *Donnie Sexton, Travel Montana*

Looking downstream from the lower of the Great Falls, the Missouri River winds away into the distance to the north. Rainbow Falls is on the left, and the smaller Crooked Falls is at the center of the islands on the right. Lewis first observed this location on June 13, 1805, and heard the thunder of the falls at least an hour before he actually saw them. *Bill Yenne*

This detail of Rainbow Falls shows how steep and high the cataracts are. The picture was taken within about a week of the same time of year that Lewis was here, so it is easy to see how the upstream hydroelectric dams control the volume of water that reaches the falls. *Bill Yenne*

approach the Columbia or not, and then be obliged to return and take the other stream would not only loose us the whole of this season but would probably so dishearten the party that it might defeat the expedition altogether."

The captains studied the two rivers intently. The north fork was deeper, but narrower. Its waters were a "whitish brown colour . . . characteristic of the Missouri; while the South fork is perfectly transparent . . . with a smoth unruffled surface. . . . The North fork gives the colouring matter and character which is retained from hence to the gulph of Mexico."

This photograph of Rainbow Falls, taken by Montana photographer Franklin Jay Haynes in 1880, clearly shows the volume of water that spilled across the falls before the dams were created. This is what Lewis and Clark saw at the Great Falls! *Haynes Foundation Collection, Montana Historical Society*

They were all certain that the north fork was correct, as was Pierre Cruzatte, whose experience as a Missouri River boatman made his opinion the most valuable. Nevertheless, Lewis and Clark dispatched a canoe and three men up each river to examine and to "find if possible which is the most probable branch." The result of this reconnaissance was the decision to take the south fork. Lewis named the other river Maria's River for his cousin Maria Wood. Through the years, the apostrophe was dropped, and it is now the "Marias," a three-syllable word ending in *us*.

The captains had been right and wrong. They chose the true Missouri, which had now turned in a southerly direction. Since their mandate from Jefferson was to follow the Missouri, this was the right path. However, the Marias would have accomplished the other mission, taking them to one of the easiest passes in the Montana Rockies where they could have crossed the Continental Divide. At its headwaters near what is now Marias Pass, they could have walked a short distance to the Middle Fork of the Flathead near the town where the author grew up. Once on the Flathead River, they would have discovered the lake of the same name, which is the largest freshwater lake in the United States west of the Great Lakes. Lewis and Clark would have had been on easily navigable waters all the way to the Columbia, although they would have reached it much farther north than they actually did. They would also have been spared the Great Falls.

The city of Great Falls, at one time Montana's largest, is named for one of those signature landmarks to which the journal-keeping captains devoted much ink.

On June 13, Lewis, who had gone ahead of the main party, was the first to see the Great Falls of the Missouri and first to understand the magnitude of this obstacle to getting all the way across the continent by boat. As Lewis first approached the Great Falls, he observed before he saw them that the "roaring [was] too tremendous to be mistaken for any cause short of the great falls of the Missouri." When he first saw them, he called them "magifficent and sublimely grand." He noted their immense size and that the bluff on which he stood "seems to reverberate."

The Lewis and Clark Scenic Overlook is located on the bluff overlooking Rainbow Falls. Fans of the Corps of Discovery expedition visit by day, and lovers find it romantic by starlight. To the captains, the view was one of the most sobering they had yet encountered. *Bill Yenne*

Black Eagle Falls is located about two miles upstream from Rainbow Falls. Black Eagle Dam is behind the falls, and parts of the city of Great Falls are visible in the distance. *Bill Yenne*

In his 1912 oil painting entitled *Lewis at Black Eagle Falls*, E. S. Paxson depicts Lewis and another man, possibly Joseph Fields, on the bluff overlooking the falls. Lewis is staring away from the river and is possibly watching out for bear. Lewis encountered a grizzly near here on June 14, 1805. *Montana Historical Society, Don Beatty*

Between Rainbow Falls and Black Eagle Falls, Lewis discovered, and was amazed by, Giant Springs, one of the largest freshwater springs in the world. It flows at a measured rate of 338 million gallons of water daily. *Bill Yenne*

The 5,500-square-foot Lewis and Clark National Historic Trail Interpretive Center is located on Giant Springs Road, which is atop the bluff a short distance downstream from Black Eagle Falls. Managed by the U.S. Forest Service, it is one of the most highly regarded centers on the Lewis and Clark trail. *Bill Yenne*

"I wished for the pencil of [Baroque master painter] Salvator Rosa," the awe-struck Lewis wrote, "that I might be enabled to give to the enlightened world some just idea of this truly magnificent and sublimely grand object, which has from the commencement of time been concealed from the view of civilized man; but this was fruitless and vain."

Based on what they had heard from the Indians they met at Fort Mandan, the Corps had anticipated a waterfall, but the Great Falls—plural—actually numbered five. Clearly, the only way around this obstacle was to walk and to carry, or portage, all of their boats and equipment by hand. Having cached their red pirogue near the mouth of the Maria's River, they decided to cache the white pirogue, along with gunpowder and other supplies, at the base of the Great Falls. The pirogue was simply too big to push up the steep banks of the Missouri and push overland. Retrieving the pirogues on the return trip would be the best plan.

The project of circumventing the falls by land filled the eight days between June 23 and the first of July with the hardest physical labor yet encountered by the Corps of Discovery. Clark observed that the men were "limping from the Soreness of their feet Some become faint for a fiew moments, but no man Complains all go Chearfully onto State the fatigues of this party would take up more of the journal than other notes." And that was on the first day of the portage. A hailstorm passed through the following day.

After the Corps manhandled all six of the Fort Mandan canoes around the Great Falls, they camped for two weeks before starting out again. At this point, Lewis unpacked the iron boat frame he had commissioned at Harpers Ferry two years earlier. His idea was

This life-size diorama inside the Lewis and Clark National Historic Trail Interpretive Center dramatically illustrates the incredibly difficult task faced by the men of the Corps of Discovery as they portaged their canoes and equipment around the Great Falls. *Donnie Sexton, Travel Montana*

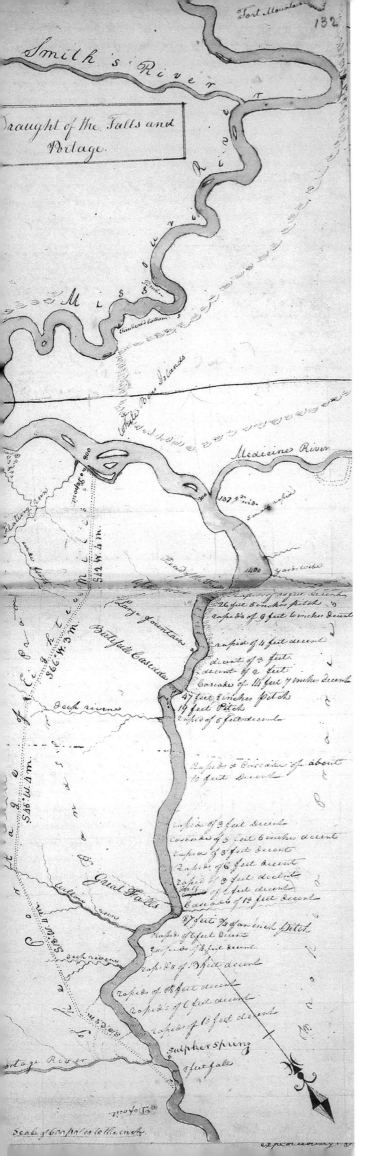

This map from the journals of Lewis and Clark charts the enormous task accomplished by the Corps of Discovery's portage around the Great Falls of the Missouri River in July 1805. *Courtesy American Philosophical Society*

that it would be covered with hides and used to carry enough to offset the absence of the pirogues they'd cached downstream of the falls. Unfortunately, he counted on adequate pine tree pitch to waterproof the boat, and there were not enough pine trees here to make this plan work. Lewis did what he could and substituted buffalo tallow for pitch. It did not work and his iron boat sank. Carried for so far, his ingenious invention was never used. He retrieved and buried the frame.

Today, the location of the iron boat is one of the enduring mysteries of the expedition. Lewis never wrote of retrieving it, so its ultimate disposition is unknown. One theory is that it was broken up, and the valuable pieces of iron were traded to the Indians. Another theory holds that it is still buried somewhere near Great Falls. However, numerous searches during the 1990s using metal detectors failed to turn up any fragment of this mother of all Lewis and Clark artifacts.

The 18-mile portage route began at Belt Creek on the southeast side of the Missouri River and roughly followed the southeast perimeter of the city limits of today's city of Great Falls. To replace the pirogue and the failed iron boat, the Corps felled two more cottonwoods and dug them out to use as canoes.

Located within the city of Great Falls, and overlooking the Missouri River above Rainbow Falls, is another of the half-dozen best interpretive centers along the trail. The 5,500-square-foot Lewis and Clark National Historic Trail Interpretive Center on Giant Springs Road is managed by the U.S. Forest Service. The highlight of the static displays is a two-story, life-size diorama depicting the men of the Corps pushing a canoe up an embankment. One can look out the window and see the scale of this task in the real embankments below. The center's theater features a 30-minute film by Ken Burns. The Lewis and Clark Institute is also housed at the Great Falls Interpretive Center and sponsors a series of field trips and workshops that explore the history, geography, natural sciences, and native cultures along the trail.

Between Loma and Great Falls, U.S. Highway 87 is the closest parallel highway to the Missouri

A Meriwether Lewis impersonator supervises the assembly of a replica of the iron boat frame during a bicentennial re-enactment at Great Falls. *Marcia Anderson, via Carol Kruger, WENDT*

The Meriwether Lewis impersonator lends a hand in completing the prow of the iron boat replica. *Marcia Anderson, via Carol Kruger, WENDT*

Whether it will work seems to perplex this Meriwether Lewis impersonator as the hides are stretched onto the iron boat frame during a bicentennial attempt to vindicate the captain's ingenious concept. *Marcia Anderson, via Carol Kruger, WENDT*

This illustration by Keith Rocco shows Meriwether Lewis and members of the Corps stretching hides to cover the iron boat frame. They used 28 elk hides and 4 buffalo hides. He planned to use pine pitch to waterproof it, but there wasn't enough available. *National Park Service, Harpers Ferry Center, artist Keith Rocco*

Upstream from Great Falls, the Missouri River meanders through some of the most beautiful countryside that Lewis and Clark had yet seen. One can imagine Lewis and Clark boating and fishing these waters, and do it in the same fashion today. *Bill Yenne*

The landscape of the Missouri River country south of Great Falls dwarfs a modern boater, just as it did the Corps of Discovery and their dugouts two centuries before. *Bill Yenne*

River. Traveling south from Great Falls, which is 2,217 miles from Camp Dubois, there are two choices. Interstate 15 follows the river more closely than many highways traveled since the Dakotas, but the frontage or recreation roads are even better.

About 35 miles and three days after departing from the Great Falls area, Clark decided to take a small group of men ashore and proceed parallel to the Missouri on foot. Although the Corps had not seen another human face since leaving Fort Mandan, there was a well-used trail along the western shore. As they neared the mountains, they knew that they were nearing the Shoshone, so it was decided that the best way to meet them as soon as possible was to proceed ashore on a well worn trail. They planned to rendezvous upstream in about a week.

A day later, on the evening of July 19, Lewis and the contingent in the canoes reached a dramatic topographical feature that Lewis identified as another geographical milestone. "This evening we entered much the most remarkable clifts that we have yet seen," he wrote. "These clifts rise from the waters edge on either side perpendicularly to the hight of 1200 feet. every object here wears a dark and gloomy aspect. the towering and projecting rocks in many places seem ready to tumble on us. the river appears to have forced it's way through this immence body of solid rock for the distance of 5 3/4 miles and where it makes it's exit below has thrown on either side vast collumns of rocks mountains high. . . . From the singular appearance of this place I called it the gates of the rocky mountains."

In fact, this canyon was merely a stand-alone feature. Since Loma, the Missouri River had turned south and was running parallel to the front range of the Rockies. Lewis'"gates of the rocky mountains" were the gates only to another broad valley that actually took the eight canoes farther from the Rockies. Exit 209 on Interstate 15, which leads to the Gates of the Mountains Recreation Area, is Milepost 2,333 on the highway trek from Camp Dubois. At the Recreation Area, boaters may recreate the voyage through the canyon that impressed Lewis, but there is no road.

Helena, Montana, the state capital, is located on Interstate 15, just 17 miles south of Exit 209. Those following the Lewis and Clark trail make this stop to view the largest, and probably the most famous, Lewis and Clark painting ever. This work by Montana artist Charles Marion Russell depicts the meeting of Lewis and Clark with the Salish people that is described in Chapter 8. By the time the eight canoes passed south of what is now the Helena area, and into the vicinity of the present Canyon Ferry Reservoir and following State Route 287, they were probably in or near the land frequented by the Shoshone, but neither Lewis nor Clark saw a soul.

Once a challenging highway into the mysterious unknown, the Missouri River is now a world-class trout stream. *Bill Yenne*

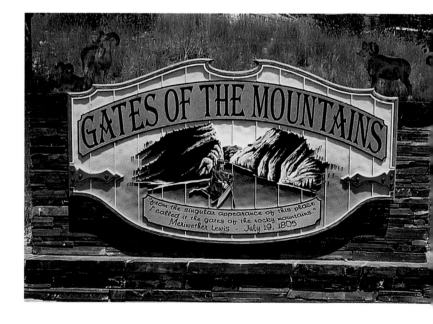

Welcome to the Gates of the Mountains. Today, the site is a recreation area where boaters routinely re-create Lewis' voyage through this anomalous, but dramatic, canyon. *Bill Yenne*

St. Louis September 23rd 1806.

It is with pleasure that I announce to you the safe arrival of myself and party at 12 OClk today at this place with our papers and baggage. In obedience to your orders we have penetrated the continent of North America to the Pacific Ocean, and sufficiently explored

of this distance 200 miles is along a good road, and 140 over tremendious mountains which for 60 mls are covered with eternal snows; however a passage over these mountains is practicable from the latter part of June to the last of September, and the cheap rate at which horses are to be obtained from the Indians of the Rocky Mountains and west of them, reduces the expences of transportation over this portage to a mere trifle. The navigation of the Kooskooske, the South East branch of the Columbia

Chapter Seven

The Headwaters

Finding the Shoshone was the necessary first step in obtaining horses, which were needed for getting across the Rockies to the Columbia. In Jefferson's mandate to Lewis, however, following the Columbia to its mouth was an objective that was secondary to finding the point where the Missouri River began.

This is the headwaters of the Missouri River. At this point, we are looking west, upriver, into the mouth of the Jefferson River, with the Madison coming in from the left. The Missouri River flows to the right and is joined by the Gallatin River a quarter-mile downstream. *Bill Yenne*

Lewis and Clark in the Old West. These signs appear along the trail, which is now the two-lane U.S. Highway 287, in Broadwater County near Townsend, Montana. Late in July 1805, Lewis and Clark passed this way and divided themselves between the trail along the shore and the Missouri River, which closely follows Highway 287. *Bill Yenne*

By July 22, near today's Townsend, Montana, at what is our modern Milepost 2,382 from Camp Dubois, Sacagawea was starting to notice familiar landmarks. She now assured Lewis that they were getting close to a place where three rivers came together to form the Missouri. Over the past thousand miles, Lewis and Clark had developed a deep respect for Sacagawea's understanding of the fabric and texture of this vast and mysterious land. She had saved their journals and she had conjured foods and medicinal herbs out of the banks of the Missouri as if by magic. Lewis had no reason to doubt the tale told of the three rivers by this 16-year-old nursing mother. It was an exciting moment.

"The Indian woman recognizes the country and assures us that this is the river on which her relations live, and that the three forks are at no great distance," Lewis wrote. "This piece of information has cheered the spirits of the party who now begin to console themselves with the anticipation of shortly seeing the head of the Missouri yet unknown to the civilized world."

On July 25, Clark and his advance party reached the headwaters of the Missouri River. On the outskirts of the conveniently named Montana town of Three Forks, three rivers of equal size flow together to form the Missouri River—the greatest tributary of the Mississippi. If the Mississippi is, as they say, the "Father of Waters," Clark now beheld the great-grandparents.

Here is the forked mouth of the Gallatin River. The Missouri River is completed as it is joined by this river a short distance downstream from the confluence of the Madison and Jefferson. The Gallatin arrives from the right, flows around the island in the center of this picture, and joins the Missouri, which flows laterally, left to right, along the base of the hills in the background. *Bill Yenne*

Leaving a note for his co-captain, Clark continued up the north fork. Although it wasn't larger than the middle fork, he decided that it "boar more to the West, and of course more in the direction we were anxious to pursue." Clark ascended this stream about 25 miles and returned to meet Lewis, who had arrived at Three Forks two days after Clark.

After climbing a prominent rock bluff to view the area, Lewis wrote in his journal that this was "an essential point in the geography of this western part of the Continent."

Downstream, the water that he observed on July 4, 1805, was the Missouri. Upstream were the "Three Forks." Lewis and Clark named the first of these for Treasury Secretary Albert Gallatin. Of the other two, the middle fork was given the name of Secretary of State and future president James Madison. The north, or west fork, which Clark had chosen for his 25-mile reconnaissance, was named for President Jefferson. Today, the Gallatin, Madison, and Jefferson forks are the holy grail of serious fly fishermen, but in 1805, the fish enjoyed the gnats and "musquitors" that drove the Corps of Discovery to distraction.

Another snow fell at Three Forks before the politicians in Washington knew that the three rivers bore their names, but the Corps of Discovery had a more immediate concern. There were an increasing number of signs that there were Shoshone people in the area. Sacagawea was anxious to be reunited with them, and Lewis and Clark were anxious to begin bartering for horses to take them across the Rockies.

On July 30, the expedition continued in a southwesterly direction following the stream they had just dubbed "Jefferson's River," now known simply as the Jefferson River. The parallel road today is State Route 41. At the town of Twin Bridges, the Jefferson River reaches its own three forks. The main route of the Jefferson River is now the Beaverhead River. The west fork, called Wisdom River by the captains, is now the Big Hole River. The east form,

The Madison River at its mouth. Here we see the river, which the captains named for the secretary of state, as they saw it in July 1805. In the distance, a late afternoon squall moves across the Madison Range of the Rockies. *Bill Yenne*

LEWIS AND CLARK AT THREE-FORKS

This 1912 oil painting by E. S Paxson, now in the Montana State Capitol in Helena, is entitled *Lewis and Clark at Three Forks*. Sacagawea is explaining the geography of the three rivers to the attentive captains. Lewis, with his three-cornered hat and telescope, is in the center, and the red-headed Clark is to his right. The man on the far right is probably Charbonneau. *Montana Historical Society, Don Beatty*

Montana has designated the confluence of the three braided rivers that form the Missouri as a state park. A large sign at the park quotes Thomas Jefferson's orders to Meriwether Lewis stating, "The object of your mission is to explore the Missouri River, and such principal streams of it, as, by its course and communication with the waters of the Pacific Ocean . . . may offer the most direct and practicable water communication across the continent." *Bill Yenne*

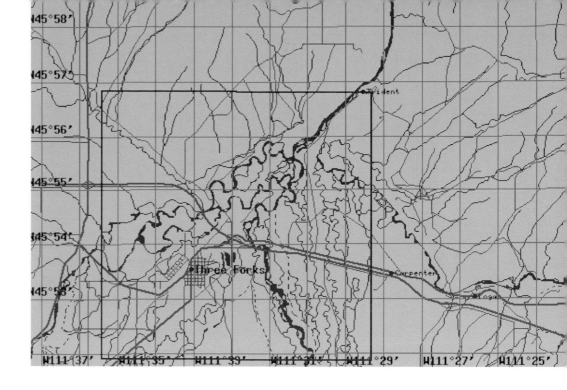

This map shows that surveying the confluence of the three rivers was not an easy task for Lewis and Clark because of the bewildering maze of tributaries and side channels. The actual confluence is just northeast of the town of Three Forks, Montana. The Jefferson arrives from the left, the Madison from the bottom, and the Gallatin from the right. The Missouri flows north at the top. *U.S. Geological Survey*

called Philanthropy River, is now the Ruby River, renamed on account of the garnet-rich ore that nineteenth-century miners once took for rubies in the rough.

On August 8, 1805, the Corps passed the cliff that the Shoshone called Beaverhead Rock, which, as Sacagawea confidently assured the captains, was an important landmark.

"The Indian woman recognized the point of a high plain to our right which she informed us was not very distant from the summer retreat of her nation on a river beyond the mountains which runs to the west," Lewis wrote. "This hill she says her nation calls the beaver's head from a conceived resemblance of it's figure to the head of that animal. she assures us that we shall either find her people on this river or on the river immediately west of it's source; which from it's present size cannot be very distant. as it is now all important with us to meet with those people as soon as possible, I determined to proceed tomorrow with a small party to the source of the principal stream of this river and pass the mountains to the Columbia; and down that river untill I found the Indians; in short it is my resolusion to find them or some others, who have horses if it should cause me a trip of one month. for without horses we shall be obliged to leave a great part of our stores, of which, it appears to me that we have a stock already sufficiently small for the length of the voyage before us."

The captains split up again. Clark was feeling "billious" and suffered from injuries to his feet from his many days of tramping along the trail ashore in thin-soled moccasins

This aerial photograph corresponds to the map at the left. Although the rivers are harder to make out, it is easier to see the topographical lay of the land at this important geographical point. Interstate 90 and the tracks operated by Montana Rail Link pass through from east to west. *U.S. Geological Survey*

Lewis and Clark opened the Northwest but railroads like this one made it great!

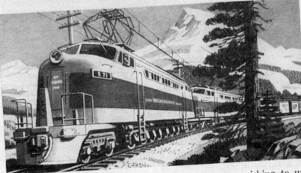

and remained behind with the majority of the Corps of Discovery, who were also ill or otherwise in need of a rest.

Lewis took George Drouillard, John Shields, and Hugh McNeal and struck out to reconnoiter the headwaters of the Jefferson River. Lewis left a note for Clark at the point where the Red Rock River and Prairie Creek flow together to form the Beaverhead and proceeded west on Prairie Creek.

On August 11, Lewis saw, through his telescope, the first human being encountered by the Corps since Fort Mandan. The lone rider disappeared, but it was presumed that he was Shoshone and that a rendezvous would soon occur. In the meantime, Lewis figured that they were truly following an active "Indian road" that would probably lead to the route across the mountains.

On August 12, the men reached the crest of a hill covered with patches of pine and stared down into the valley beyond. This was it. At the 7,373-foot crest of what is now Lemhi Pass, they had reached the Continental Divide and looked for the first time into the vast land drained by the Columbia, rather than the Missouri. As numerous dramatizations of this moment have underscored, Lewis beheld not a long gentle slope leading straight to the Pacific Ocean, but the most rugged terrain yet beheld in North America by a person born in the United States.

In 1955, the Chicago, Milwaukee, St. Paul, & Pacific Railroad used Lewis and Clark in their advertising. The Milwaukee Road did not follow the Lewis and Clark trail, but crossed it at several places, including Three Forks, Montana. It is interesting to note that the artist took a bit of license and depicted the captains with cowboy hats and gave their canoe a sleek, smooth prow. *Author collection*

"We proceeded on to the top of the dividing ridge from which I discovered immence ranges of high mountains [the Bitterroot Range] still to the West of us with their tops partially covered with snow," Lewis wrote. "I now decended the mountain about 3/4 of a mile which I found much steeper than on the opposite side, to a handsome bold running Creek [today known as Agency Creek] of cold Clear water. here I first tasted the water of the great Columbia river."

It would not be until the following day that Lewis finally made contact with the Shoshone. They had never seen Euro-Americans before and were suspicious that Lewis' party was somehow associated with their mortal enemies from the northern plains, the Blackfeet. Lewis successfully convinced the Shoshone Chief Cameahwait of their peaceful intentions, and the Shoshone shared a meal with the hungry men. Over the coming days, Drouillard impressed and delighted the Shoshone with his ability to hunt deer with a musket.

Cameahwait agreed that he and other Shoshone would accompany Lewis back to the place where he had left the note for Clark, hoping that his co-captain would be there by now. He was not, but Lewis managed to convince the Shoshone to wait. The canoes finally arrived on August 17, but Charbonneau and Sacagawea were walking ahead and arrived shortly ahead of Clark and the main party. When Sacagawea came face to face with Cameahwait, she realized that he was her brother!

This happy coincidence made the already congenial relations between the Corps and the Shoshone even better. Together, more than 50 Shoshone made camp alongside the Corps at the place where the Jefferson River officially began. To celebrate everyone's good fortune, the captains named the place Camp Fortunate. Located at Milepost 2,543 from Camp Dubois, Camp Fortunate is 18 miles south of the Dillon, the seat of Beaverhead County, on Interstate 15. Unfortunately, it is also about 147 feet under the waters of the reservoir backed up behind Clark Canyon Dam. Constructed between 1961 and 1964, the dam has the distinction of being aligned on the 45th parallel, halfway between the equator and the north pole. Signs at the site commemorate Camp Fortunate and point to the reservoir.

Although the Shoshone themselves were short on food and other supplies, they were generous with the Corps of Discovery, and vice versa. The Corps had little, and the Shoshone even less, but they shared. In revisionist history, we learn that the first Thanksgiving at Plymouth, Massachusetts, was an apocryphal event and that the affable cooperation we celebrate is a myth. Celebrating the real events of August 1805 at Camp Fortunate would be closer to the Thanksgiving myth. Arrangements were made for the Corps to trade for the best 30 horses the Shoshone could spare. With Sacagawea present as a translator, they were able to discuss a route across the mountain range that Lewis had seen from the top of Lemhi Pass, the one beyond, and those beyond that. What Lewis and Clark learned was sobering. The mountains were steep, the timber was thick, and the game was scarce.

The Shoshone themselves had never been all the way across these mountains, but they had traded with the Nez Perce, who lived on the other side, and the Shoshone said the Nez Perce crossed these mountains regularly to hunt buffalo on the plains. This proved that crossing the mountains was possible, so Lewis and Clark were cautiously

A Sacagawea impersonator closely examines some beadwork at a bicentennial re-enactment. The real Sacagawea's attention to detail proved of immeasurable value to the success of the Lewis and Clark expedition. *Marcia Anderson, via Carol Kruger, WENDT*

Just like the real Meriwether Lewis, this bicentennial re-enactor came equipped with his sextant for a precise reading of his location. In the hands of a skilled navigator, a sextant can be almost as accurate as a modern GPS device. The sextant readings of Lewis and Clark provided the essential data for generations of cartographers. *Marcia Anderson, via Carol Kruger, WENDT*

On August 8, 1805, Sacagawea recognized this mountain from her childhood and knew that she was near Shoshone land. It still is known as Beaverhead Rock because of, in Lewis' words, "A conceived resemblance of it's figure to the head of that animal." As with Lewis, most people cannot make out the resemblance. The portion of Jefferson River seen in the foreground has long since been renamed the Beaverhead River. *Donnie Sexton, Travel Montana*

By the time they reached this point on "Jefferson's River," now the Beaverhead River, on August 10, 1805, the Corps of Discovery dragged its canoes. Clark, along with Sacagawea and Charbonneau, walked on shore, and Lewis had already gone ahead to scout a pass across the Continental Divide. *Bill Yenne*

optimistic. In addition to the horses, Cameahwait agreed to send with them an old Shoshone man who was believed to know more about the trails that crossed the mountains than any other member of the tribe. The captains nicknamed him "Toby" because part of his name sounded like "Shoshone."

It was clearly impossible to portage the canoes over the mountains they now faced, so the Corps cached them at Camp Fortunate and planned to build new ones as soon as they crossed the divide a week or so later. It was wishful thinking. Nearly two months of profoundly difficult travel lay ahead before the Corps was able once again to put canoes into the water.

In his 1988 oil painting entitled *At Lemhi*, Robert F. Morgan depicts Meriwether Lewis at what is now Lemhi Pass. Along with George Drouillard, Hugh McNeal, and John Shields, Lewis surveys the mountains to the west from the crest of the Continental Divide. Lewis and his party reached this point on August 12, 1805. *Montana Historical Society, John Reddy*

Three young Montana re-enactors stand ready to re-create the Lewis and Clark experience. *Marcia Anderson, via Carol Kruger, WENDT*

Lemhi Pass, as it appeared in May 1953, is still one of the most remote crossings of the Continental Divide accessible by automobile. The 7,373-foot pass marks the boundary between Montana and Idaho. *Reverend M. J. McPike*

Ada McPike takes a sip of water from the spring that Lewis called the most "distant spring of the mighty Missouri." This spring is the source of Prairie Creek that flows together with the Red Rock River to form the Beaverhead River ("Jefferson's River"). Geographers now insist that the Red Rock River, not Prairie Creek, is the true source of the Missouri, but the spring pictured here is closer to the Continental Divide. *Reverend M. J. McPike*

A modern hiker crosses Lemhi Pass. Lewis first reached the pass on August 12, 1805, and went back and recrossed it two weeks later. Clark crossed the pass on August 19. Neither captain came this way in 1806. *Donnie Sexton, Travel Montana*

Since 1964, the Camp Fortunate Overlook has looked over the Clark Canyon Reservoir. The historic point where Sacagawea was reunited with her brother and where Lewis and Clark counseled with the Shoshone is 147 feet below the surface. *Bill Yenne*

The landscape at Lemhi Pass is shown here ablaze with the color of spring wildflowers. As with many of the landscapes that Lewis and Clark saw, the view is essentially unchanged. *Donnie Sexton, Travel Montana*

This painting by Charles Marion Russell, simply entitled *Lewis and Clark Expedition*, depicts Sacagawea being reunited with her family near the site of what was named Camp Fortunate. William Clark takes center stage, but his eyes are fixed on the Shoshone teenager as she embraces another woman who, Lewis wrote, "had been taken prisoner at the same time with her, and who had afterwards escaped." The man in the red cap is probably Toussaint Charbonneau, and the mounted Shoshone man gesturing with his hands is probably Chief Cameahwait, Sacagawea's brother. Note the snow-capped Bitterroots beckoning from the distance. This painting is in the collection of the Gilcrease Museum in Tulsa, Oklahoma. *Gilcrease Museum*

This display commemorates the fortunate meeting with the Shoshone that allowed the Corps of Discovery to obtain the horses they needed to cross the Rocky Mountains. *Bill Yenne*

This tepee in Gallatin County, Montana, is typical of those traditionally used by the people of the plains, as well as by those living in the Great Basin, such as the Shoshone. *Bill Yenne*

St. Louis September 23rd 1806.

It is with pleasure that I announce to you the safe arrival of myself and party at 12 OClock today at this place with our papers and baggage. In obedience to your orders we have penetrated the continent of North America to the Pacific Ocean, and sufficiently explored

posed across the continent; of this distance 200 miles is along a good road, and 140 over tremendious mountains which for 60 ms are covered with eternal snows; however a passage over these mountains is practicable from the latter part of June to the last of September, and the cheap rate at which horses are to be obtained from the Indians of the Rocky Mountains and West of them, reduce the expences of transportation over this portage to a mere trifle. the navigation of the Kooskooske, the South East branch of the

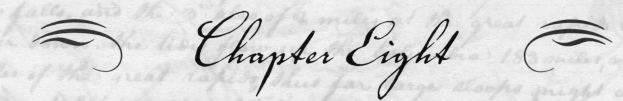

Chapter Eight

"Within the Bosom of This Wild and Mountainous Country"

T his July 1805 quote from Meriwether Lewis clearly describes the lives of the Corps of Discovery through the late summer and autumn of that year. Accompanied by Charbonneau, Sacagawea, Toby, and several members of the Corps of Discovery, William Clark crossed the Continental Divide on August 19, 1805, at Lemhi Pass, the same crossing point that Lewis had used a week earlier. Lewis recrossed here on August 26 with the rest of the Corps. Both parties were accompanied by members of the Shoshone tribe.

The Bitterroot River passes through a broad, level valley that gave the Corps of Discovery a week of respite between the extreme difficulty of Lost Trail Pass and the horror of climbing across Lolo Pass. *Bill Yenne*

Old Toby, the Shoshone guide that accompanied Lewis and Clark in September 1805, is said to have had trouble finding the route across the mountains into the Bitterroot Valley. Today, two-lane U.S. Highway 93 winds its way to the top of the pass named for his alleged lapses in trail-blazing skills. The pass also marks the border between Idaho and Montana. *Bill Yenne*

The steep terrain on Lost Trail Pass made travel difficult for the Corps of Discovery in 1805 and for road-builders a century later. *Bill Yenne*

Reachable now only by a treacherous gravel road, the pass is Milepost 2,573 from Camp Dubois. Today, this section of the divide forms the border between Montana and Idaho. The remoteness and difficulty of the pass more than 200 years after Lewis and Clark underscores what it must have been like for them. This is confirmation of how truly remote most of the Lewis and Clark trail still is.

Clark had gone ahead and assumed that he would be able to find both a navigable river and cottonwoods from which to build dugout canoes. Having reached the Salmon River south of the present Idaho town of the same name, Clark explored its main fork. Staring slack jawed at the formidable rapids that frighten river rafters to this day, he decided to abandon this course for another. Toby insisted that the place where the Nez Perce crossed the mountains was farther north.

As the Corps followed the north fork of the Salmon River, they beheld a dizzying maze of ridges, box canyons, and almost impossibly steep hillsides. Even the rudest of pessimists could not have imagined that the Corps of Discovery now faced hundreds of miles of the most rugged terrain any of them had seen. This is not to mention that they had to climb another pass with an elevation in the vicinity of 7,000 feet. These days, vehicles ascending the pass from the south on U.S. Highway 93 find the climb to be an arduous one that requires frequent downshifting.

To make matters worse for the Corps, even Toby got lost. The pass where they crossed back into Montana is now called Lost Trail Pass in commemoration of this less than fortunate moment in the annals of the Corps of Discovery, although the name wasn't coined until early in the twentieth century.

Once across the pass, Lewis and Clark followed the route of today's Highway 93 northward. Reaching the broad valley that was named Ross' Hole, they began following the course of the east fork of the Bitterroot River. It was also at Ross' Hole, near the present settlement of Sula, Montana, that they made contact with the second tribe they would meet in the Rockies. These people, whom the captains incorrectly identified as Flathead, were the Salish, who did not practice the custom of flattening the heads of their babies. They were allies of the Shoshone, and the two tribes often banded together for an annual buffalo hunt east of the Rockies. The Salish lived in the valleys to the north, which are now known as the Bitterroot, Jocko, Mission, and Flathead.

Clark noted that the Salish people "recved us friendly, threw white robes over our

Sholders & Smoked in the pipes of peace, we Encamped with them & found them friendly but nothing but berries to eate a part of which they gave us." It is this meeting, which occurred on September 4, that is celebrated by Charles Russell's great painting in the State Capitol in Helena.

The Salish had about 500 head of horses, mostly of a higher quality than the Shoshone horses, and Lewis and Clark were able to trade up and replace some of their more marginal stock for the trek ahead. For the moment, this trip was a relatively easy one as the Corps followed the broadening valley of the Bitterroot River—the Corps named it the Flathead River in honor of their name for the Salish—north along the route of today's U.S. Highway 93. Today's Flathead River is an unrelated river more than 100 miles to the north. Accompanied by the Salish, they covered what is today about 70 highway miles in five days.

On September 9, 1805, about a dozen miles short of the present Missoula city limits, the Corps and the Salish made camp on Lolo Creek, which Lewis described as "a handsome stream about 100 yards wide and affords a considerable quantity of very clear water."

On September 4, 1805, Lewis and Clark arrived in the broad valley, or "hole," that was later named for Alexander Ross of the Hudson Bay Company. *Bill Yenne*

Lewis dubbed the location "Travelers' Rest." Travelers had been resting here for centuries because the trail that crosses the Bitterroot Range to the rivers that flow into the Columbia River follows Lolo Creek west from here. Lewis and Clark and their party were the first travelers of European descent to rest in this meadow.

During the summer of 2002, archaeologist Dan Hall discovered the Corps of Discovery's campsite at Travelers' Rest, making it the only place on the entire 8,000-mile route where there is incontrovertible forensic evidence of the precise location of a Lewis and Clark camp. The location of their main cooking fire was found and the charcoal was carbon dated to the turn of the nineteenth century. A cooking fire could have belonged to anyone camping here around that time, and evidence shows camps in the area dating back to the tenth century B.C. However, a U.S. Army contingent, such as the Corps of Discovery, would have followed certain conventions when making their camp. Hall knew that the U.S. Army of 1804–1806 used the Revolutionary War-era field manual edited by Baron Frederick Wilhelm von Steuben. Such a manual contained specifications for every aspect of military activities, including the layout of encampments. In this case, Hall knew that the manual dictated that the latrine of an encampment was to be 300 feet downhill and downstream from the cooking fire. At Traveler's Rest, Hall found evidence of a trench 300 feet downhill and downstream from the cooking fire.

Investigating this trench, Hall discovered large concentrations of mercury in the center and none a short distance away. Because several members of the expedition were ill during the stay and were taking Dr. Rush's purgative pills, the high levels of mercury confirmed the trench as the Corps' latrine.

Charles Marion Russell's legendary painting entitled *Lewis and Clark Meeting the Indians at Ross' Hole* is one of the most important paintings ever done of the expedition. Russell deliberately made the Salish horsemen, rather than the captains, the center of attention. Measuring 296 by 140 inches, the work resides behind the speaker's desk in the house chambers at the State Capitol. It depicts the meeting of Lewis and Clark with the Salish in September 1805. Russell received the commission from the state legislature in 1911 and finished the painting in July 1912, two months before his deadline. As tour guides point out when they show the painting, the dog in the center looks directly upon the speaker's podium. *Montana Historical Society, Don Beatty*

Further archeological investigations have turned up a metal button and a blue trading bead, and both are of the type that would have been present in the Corps' supplies. Also found was a musket ball and melted lead comprised of a lead isotope traceable to the Olive Mine in northern Kentucky. Lewis acquired the expedition supplies in northern Kentucky.

"The latrine has the ability to stand on its own as proof," Hall said. "But when combined with everything else, it is bulletproof. There is more evidence here than anywhere else on the trail. This is a place of stories, and whether large or small, old or new, they are stories not found anywhere else."

The site is preserved as Travelers' Rest State Park and managed by the nonprofit Travelers' Rest Preservation and Heritage Association.

On September 11, 1805, Lewis and Clark left Travelers' Rest and followed Lolo Creek to the west. Nine months later, on June 30, 1806, they returned to rest and begin separate eastward treks across Montana that took them to entirely new places in the Big Sky Country.

As they headed up Lolo Creek from their pleasant campsite, they were in for the most difficult traveling they had yet seen. The easy stroll through the Bitterroot Valley from Ross' Hole had been parallel to the Bitterroot Range. Now they were crossing these mountains and encountering the same sort of near-vertical terrain that they'd seen between Lemhi and Lost Trail Pass. To make matters worse, less than a week after leaving Travelers' Rest, they were traveling in snow.

At first, the trip didn't seem so bad. Two days out of Travelers Rest, they were basking in the mineral baths at today's Lolo Hot Springs, where Clark observed that the "Indians had made a [hole] to bathe." He tasted this water and found it "nearly boiling hot at the places it Spouted from the rocks."

Leaving the hot springs, old Toby "took a wrong road and took us out of our rout 3 miles through intolerable [terrain]." They got back on track, but this was only the beginning. The next day, as they passed the summit of mile-high Lolo Pass, snowflakes were in the air.

Lolo Pass marks Milepost 2,673 from Camp Dubois and also marks both the Idaho state line and the beginning of a direct water route to the Columbia River. From here, the Lochsa River flows to the Clearwater, to the Snake, and finally the great Columbia. Of course, the Corps of Discovery was not afloat again for two terrible weeks.

Their route, which now parallels U.S. Highway 12, is generally followed by a dirt and gravel rut known as the "Lolo Motorway" that warps and turns for more than 100 excruciating miles across numberless ridges. It is the most difficult part of the Lewis and Clark trail and is often abandoned by modern travelers in favor of twisting, two-lane Highway 12, which is itself far from being a superhighway. This terrain is so rough that Highway 12 itself, known alternately as the Lewis and Clark Highway, was under construction for decades and not completed until 1962.

In 1805, the hardship of the land was magnified by the fact that the game had abandoned the high country by September, and the expedition's hunters came up empty handed. The

Autumn on the Bitterroot River was captured in this photo in late September 1952. When Lewis and Clark passed this way 147 years earlier, the fall colors may not have been quite as advanced, but for them, the first heavy snowfall was only a week away.
Reverend M. J. McPike

This is the only scientifically confirmed exact location of a Lewis and Clark encampment. People had settled in the area west of Lolo, Montana, through the years, but the actual campsite remained virtually untouched. *Bill Yenne*

Corps was forced to start eating their horses and chewing on tallow candles as they struggled through deepening snow. The last of their several glass thermometers had broken, so the temperature was impossible to pinpoint, but Clark did observe that "I was at one time fearfull my feet would freeze in the thin mockersons which I wore."

Their difficulties in the mountains may have seemed interminable, but it lasted just a few days. On September 20, Clark and John Colter led an advance party out of the steepest part of the mountains and into the meadow now known as the Weippe Prairie. Here, he found an encampment of the Nez Perce (Pierced Nose) living there in the drainage of the Clearwater River. These people routinely made the crossing that the Corps of Discovery had just accomplished. The Nez Perce had to have been surprised to find these fools attempting this feat so late in the year.

"The Chopunnish or Pierced nose Indians are Stout likeley men, handsom women, and verry dressey in their way," Clark observed. "Their amusements appear but fiew as their Situation requires the utmost exertion to procure food they are generally employed in that pursute, all the Summer & fall fishing for the Salmon, the winter hunting the deer on Snow Shoes in the plains and taking care of their emence numbers of horses, & in the Spring cross the mountains to the Missouri to get Buffalow robes and [meat]."

Shown here is an overview of the meadow at Travelers' Rest. The horses probably grazed in this area. It has been confirmed that the main cooking fire was located on the left, just beyond the trees. *Bill Yenne*

This is the location of the trench that was dug by the Corps of Discovery for the latrine. The high concentrations of mercury in this soil confirm it was used by the Corps. *Bill Yenne*

Of all the hospitable tribes that Lewis and Clark encountered during their two-way trek across the continent, there is perhaps none that fits the bill for being a participant in a real model for the "First Thanksgiving" than the Nez Perce. Like the Shoshone, they shared food when food was scarce, and they shared precious horses. By the time the Corps of Discovery reached Nez Perce country, they were on the edge of starvation. The hospitality of the Nez

Snowcapped Lolo Peak could be seen in the distance from Travelers' Rest in 1805. The snow was more ominous than they probably realized. The pine may date from before 1805. Other trees at Travelers' Rest have been confirmed to have been present when Lewis and Clark slept there. *Bill Yenne*

Lolo Creek, upstream from the Bitterroot River, is a pleasant little brook, but not navigable. By this time, the Corps members traveled mostly on foot and used their horses as pack animals. *Bill Yenne*

Perce saved lives and perhaps helped ensure the success of the Lewis and Clark expedition. On September 22, Lewis wrote that they had "tryumphed over the rockey Mountins."

The Corps camped with the Nez Perce for several days and presented Jefferson peace medals to leaders, including Twisted Hair, and arranged to have their horses "boarded" here through the winter. They cached supplies on the Clearwater River, which they called the "Kooskooske" after the Nez Perce name for it, and began constructing canoes. During the first week of October, the Corps of Discovery put into the river near the present town of Orofino, Idaho, which marks Milepost 3,049 from Camp Dubois.

For roadside businesses along the Lolo Trail (U.S. Highway 12), the folklore of the Lewis and Clark is never far from mind. *Bill Yenne*

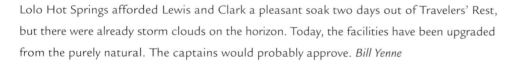

Lolo Hot Springs afforded Lewis and Clark a pleasant soak two days out of Travelers' Rest, but there were already storm clouds on the horizon. Today, the facilities have been upgraded from the purely natural. The captains would probably approve. *Bill Yenne*

Opened in June 2003, the Lolo Pass Visitor Center was a joint project between the U.S. Forest Service and the transportation departments of Montana and Idaho. Lolo Pass marks the boundary between the two states, as well as the boundary between the Lolo National Forest (to the east) and the Clearwater National Forest (to the west). *Bill Yenne*

This sign on Lolo Pass commemorates the first crossing by men from the eastern United States. The native people of the West had used the pass for more than a century. *Bill Yenne*

In the state of Idaho, the signs that mark U.S. Highway 12 (a.k.a the Lewis and Clark Highway) are color-coded in brown to identify the road as a historic highway. *Bill Yenne*

The Lewis and Clark Highway drops down into Idaho from the top of Lolo Pass and winds through the mountains of the Clearwater National Forest. *Bill Yenne*

Left: In 1805, Lewis and Clark faced the horror of deep snow in the Bitterroots. Curly Klauss pauses here during a hunting trip about 150 years later. Deep snow still characterizes late fall in the Bitterroots, but on a sunny day, the view is more pleasing than frightening. *Curly Klauss Collection*

Below: The rocky slopes and steep hillsides in the mountains west of Lolo Pass would make travel difficult even in the best of weather. *Bill Yenne*

Below: The nearly vertical terrain of the Idaho panhandle is reminiscent of Chinese landscape paintings that represent areas such as the Guangxi Province. *Bill Yenne*

The Lochsa River twists its way through the Idaho panhandle. Lewis and Clark passed this way, but they were still afoot in the mountains because the river is too rocky late in the season to be useful for dugout canoes. *Bill Yenne*

The pleasant meadows west of the mountains were a welcome relief after the difficult struggle on the steep, slippery cliffs above. It was here that Lewis and Clark finally made contact with the Nez Perce. *Bill Yenne*

The Happy Canyon Princess flashes a friendly smile as she rides in a parade on the Nez Perce Reservation in 1985. The friendliness of the Nez Perce contributed greatly to the success of the Lewis and Clark expedition. *Bill Yenne*

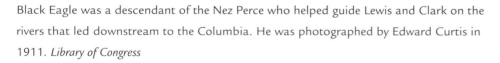

Black Eagle was a descendant of the Nez Perce who helped guide Lewis and Clark on the rivers that led downstream to the Columbia. He was photographed by Edward Curtis in 1911. *Library of Congress*

Chapter Nine

Through the Gorge to the Mouth of the Columbia

By October 7, 1805, the Corps of Discovery was once again afloat and now accompanied by Nez Perce guides. That first morning on the Clearwater River, the Corps experienced an all-new phenomenon. They were back on the water, but this time they were traveling with the current, rather than against it, and they knew this would be the case until they reached their goal. Although they encountered a number of problematic rapids, their progress was much faster than it had been on the Missouri.

The cottonwoods still grow along the banks of the Clearwater River near where the Corps of Discovery felled trees to make canoes in 1805. *Bill Yenne*

Following the river on U.S. Highway 12, it is 36 miles from Orofino, Idaho, to the place where the Clearwater empties into the Snake River on the border between Idaho and Washington state. The confluence is commemorated by naming the border twin cities Lewiston, Idaho, and Clarkston, Washington.

As is the case with the Missouri River in eastern Montana, no modern roads follow the Snake River in eastern Washington after U.S. Highway 12 leaves its banks about 10 miles west of Clarkston at Chief Timothy State Park. At Waitsburg, State Route 124 continues west to revisit the Snake and rejoin Highway 12 at Burbank, 128 highway miles from Clarkston. At Burbank, the road crosses the last mile of the Snake, entering Washington's Tri-Cities of Pasco, Kennewick, and Richland.

Upon reaching the Clearwater River near Weippe Prairie, Lewis and Clark had crossed the Continental Divide, and at last, they were traveling along a navigable river in the downstream direction. Bill Yenne

An important difference between these two experiences was that, while the Corps had traveled the Missouri and the Jefferson across Montana for four months without seeing anyone on the shore, they observed people watching from the shore almost the entire distance from Orofino to the Tri-Cities.

The Corps now met a new tribe of indigenous people nearly every day. These people were naturally wary of strangers, but when they saw Sacagawea and Pompey, they were

Right: West of the present town of Orofino, Idaho, the captains decided it was time to get back into the water. The approximate site of the camp where they dug out cottonwood logs to build canoes for their trip to the Columbia River is memorialized at this wayside along U.S. Highway 12. *Bill Yenne*

Left: Known to the Nez Perce and to Lewis and Clark as the "Kooskooske," the Clearwater River was the first navigable river that the Corps of Discovery had traveled since they left Jefferson's River two months before. *Bill Yenne*

much more at ease. The people knew that it was unlikely that the strangers were a threat because war parties usually didn't travel with a nursing mother and her baby. "We find [Sacagawea's presence] reconciles all the Indians, as to our friendly intentions," Clark wrote on October 13. "A woman with a party of men is a token of peace."

As they moved downstream, the captains also made note of a change in the basic economy of the people. The Nez Perce were hunters who valued their horses, while the downstream tribes relied much more on fishing, because game was scarce, and seemed to have little need for horses. The Corps bartered for salmon, but by now, the hungry men were also eating dogs, a meat for which they were developing a great fondness.

On October 17, the Corps camped on the grounds of what is now Pasco's 284-acre Sacajawea State Park, overlooking the confluence of the Snake and Columbia rivers. Ten days after entering the Clearwater at Orofino, Lewis and Clark reached the West's largest river. Here, they counseled with the Walla Walla people living in what is now Pasco. "The principal Chief came down with Several of his principal men and Smoked with us," Clark wrote. "Several men and woman offered Dogs and fish to Sell, we purchased all the dogs we could, the fish being out of Season."

When they finally entered the Columbia River, the Corps of Discovery found themselves on the broadest river that they had seen since the Mississippi, a sight that is still impressive today.

About 25 miles south of the Tri-Cities, the south-flowing Columbia makes an abrupt turn to the west, and from here to its mouth, it forms the boundary between Washington and Oregon. In Oregon, the river is followed by U.S. Highway 730 west through Umatilla. This highway intersects Interstate 84 and the contiguous U.S. Highway 30 about 35 miles west of the Oregon state line. The interstate closely follows the river from here to near Portland, a distance of more than 160 miles. Interstate 84 ends at Portland, but Highway 30 continues to follow the river to the mouth of the Columbia. On the Washington side, State Route 14 follows the Columbia from Plymouth, opposite Umatilla, to Vancouver, which is opposite Portland.

The course of the Columbia between Umatilla and Portland is one of the most dramatic riverscapes to be seen on the Lewis and Clark trail. Over the centuries, the Columbia has cut itself into a deep, broad gorge that runs through a vast and arid desert plateau. The toast-colored hills

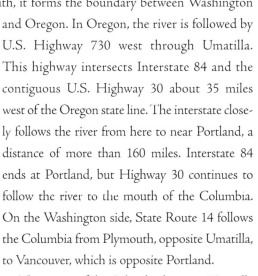

Lewis and Clark slept here. Actually, they slept near here, but the accommodations were a bit more primitive in 1805. *Bill Yenne*

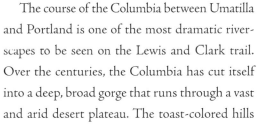

Sacagawea slept near here. This motel in Lewiston, Idaho, is one of many places of business named for the Shoshone teenager across the West. The "Sacajawea" spelling was common for most of the two centuries after her death in 1812. *Bill Yenne*

The mouth of the Clearwater River can be seen in the center of this photograph. The Snake River flows from right to left. The picture was taken from Clarkston, Washington, looking across the Snake at Lewiston, Idaho. *Bill Yenne*

they saw here was a stark contrast to the foggy and perpetually rainy climate that the Corps of Discovery discovered near the mouth of the Columbia.

Across the southern side of the gorge, U.S. Highway 30 and Interstate 84 today follow the course of the legendary Oregon Trail, the famous thoroughfare used by countless immigrants who had been encouraged by Lewis and Clark's bold trek westward.

If the Corps of Discovery looked forward to a relatively easy float from here to the Pacific, they were disappointed. The waterway was filled with treacherous rapids and falls. Many of these have since been mollified by a series of hydroelectric dams that were built during the middle of the twentieth century for the federal government's Bonneville Power Administration.

This is where the Snake meets the Columbia. The U.S. Highway 12 bridge crosses the mouth of the Snake River near Pasco, Washington. On the left is Pasco's Sacajawea Park, where the Corps of Discovery spent two nights in October 1805. *Bill Yenne*

The huge Columbia River is pictured here as it is seen just west of Umatilla, Oregon. The state of Washington is on the opposite bank, and the Union Pacific Railroad tracks cut though the sagebrush in the foreground. Lewis and Clark encountered numerous villages of native people along the river. *Bill Yenne*

Unlike the dams on the Missouri River, these dams have not backed up vast lakes, but they have submerged many of the rapids and falls that Lewis and Clark noted. Among these is Celilo Falls, near Wishram, Washington. Called the "Great Falls of the Columbia" by Clark, they remained as such until they were, in the words of a U.S. Geologic Survey report, drowned in 1957 by the Dalles Dam. In 1804, Lewis and Clark observed the local Wishram and Yakima people catching salmon as they transited these falls. Also noted were huge racks that were used for drying the fish as they were caught. The site remained an important fishery for the native people of the area until the dam was built.

The Wishram, whom Lewis and Clark called Echelute, helped the Corps portage around Celilo Falls and traded one of their canoes to Clark. He described his new acquisition as being "neeter made [than the expedition canoes] and Calculated to ride the waves, and carry emence burthens." Better-constructed Indian canoes were seen as the Corps neared the ocean.

A few miles downstream, at the Dalles, near the modern Oregon city of the same name, the Corps encountered the quarter-mile long Short Narrows that Clark called an "agitated

As one moves downstream through the Columbia Gorge, the terrain is characterized by high cliffs near the river. Interstate 84 closely follows the Columbia River through the gorge. Most of the Lewis and Clark trail is not followed by interstate highways. *Bill Yenne*

Windsurfers catch the wind on the deep waters upstream from the Dalles Dam. This was the home of Celilo Falls before the dam was built, when the Columbia still ran free. *Bill Yenne*

Salmon fishing at Celilo Falls was a big production until 1957, when the Dalles Dam was completed. This photograph shows numerous fishermen at work during salmon season in the 1930s. *Library of Congress*

gut swelling, boiling & whorling in every direction." Below that was three miles of the equally dangerous Long Narrows. After a three-day respite at Fort Rock, they tackled the final obstacle, the Cascades, which is four continuous miles of chutes and falls that required two days to descend. All of these have since been submerged because of the dams.

Today in this section of the Columbia, numerous opportunities are offered by entrepreneurs with various types of watercraft—from barges to party boats—for Lewis and Clark buffs to recapture the magic of sailing on the Columbia.

By the first of November, the Corps was below the Dalles and started to see evidence that they were, at last, nearing the waters of the Pacific Ocean. They started to experience thick fog and see occasional sea lions and sea otters. The Corps also now saw the large and elaborately constructed ocean-going canoes sailed by people from the Chinook-speaking coastal tribes.

Two months before, Lewis and Clark had met the Salish and had called them "Flathead." Now they were meeting the tribes that actually did follow the practice of using cradleboards to flatten the heads of their children. Clark also referred to these people as "Flathead" without commenting on the many cultural differences between them and the Salish.

These people whom they met ashore in the numerous villages that lined the banks of this section of the Columbia had beads and metal trade goods that were of European origin. They had gotten these either directly or indirectly from American or British ships that had called at the mouth of the Columbia. When Jefferson and Lewis planned the expedition more than two years earlier, they had discussed a rendezvous at the mouth of the Columbia with such a ship.

At Portland, the Columbia River intersects the Willamette River, which Lewis and Clark named Multnomah, after the local branch of the Chinook people. From here, the Columbia curves north for about 40 miles before bending west again at Longview, Washington, for its final path to its mouth.

On November 7, Clark recorded the day as beginning with a cloudy, foggy morning, and the Corps traveled 34 miles, despite stopping at a village to trade for some fish and dogs. That night, they found themselves camping within earshot of the Pacific Ocean.

"Great joy in camp," Clark wrote. "We are in View of the Ocian, this great Pacific [Ocean] which we been So long anxious to See. and the roreing or noise made by the waves brakeing on the rockey Shores (as I Suppose) may be heard distinctly."

The joy soon evaporated as the Corps made camp. "Scercely room Suffient for us all to lie Clear of the tide water." Clark complained. "Hills high & with a Steep assent, river wide & at this place too Salt to be used for Drink. we are all wet and disagreeable."

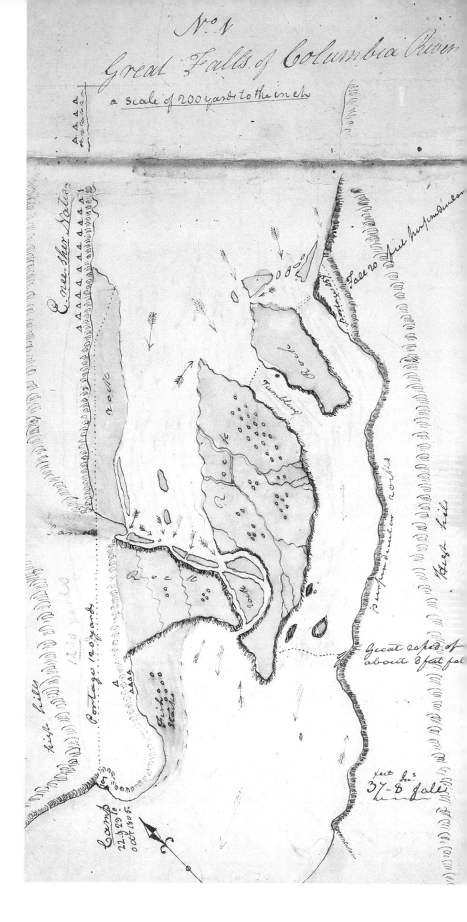

This map from the journals of Lewis and Clark describes the portage around Celilo Falls in October 1805.
Courtesy American Philosophical Society

WISHRAM GIRL

WISHRAM BRIDE

Face piercing was practiced by this young Wishram bride. The Wishram lived in the vicinity of Celilo Falls and helped the Corps of Discovery quickly make their portage around the so-called "Great Falls of the Columbia." *Library of Congress*

Customs and costumes among the Wishram people had changed little between the time of Lewis and Clark's visit and when this girl was photographed by Edward Curtis a century later. Even in 1805, beads, bangles, and other European trade goods had made their way upriver from ships visiting the mouth of the Columbia. *Library of Congress*

They were near Gray's Point in Washington, across the Columbia from modern day Astoria, Oregon. The present city itself is a monument to western settlement and named for John Jacob Astor, the wealthy industrialist who was inspired by the Lewis and Clark expedition to construct a fur trading settlement on the site. Oregon is still officially nicknamed "the Beaver State."

The next step, because they were so close, was to actually reach the ocean, both for the satisfaction of having done it and the hope of making contact with a ship. The local Chinook people living there told them there were trading ships anchored at Baker Bay, which was on the maps Lewis carried. Unfortunately, the season had advanced to the point where it was virtually impossible to get safely past the bar that separated the Columbia from the ocean. No sailing ship captain was likely to risk his vessel and crew trying to enter the Columbia until the spring.

The Corps didn't reach the ocean by canoe. Because of the powerful ocean tides and the massive waves, it took three days for the Corps to advance a few miles to what they called Point Distress—today the northern end of the U.S. Highway 101 bridge—and another five to reach Baker Bay, a dozen miles away and just inside the mouth of the river. "The Swells were So high and the Canoes roled in Such a manner as to cause Several to be verry Sick," Clark wrote on November 8. "Reubin fields, Wiser, McNeal & [Sacagawea] wer of the number." Winter had come to the Pacific Northwest.

Despite the waves and wind, not to mention hailstorms and huge cedar logs thrown at their camp by the tidal action, Lewis and Clark were still anxious to reach the Pacific. "Not withstanding the disagreeable time of the party for Several days past," Clark wrote. "[We] are all Chearfull and full of anxiety to See further into the ocian."

The port and industrial city of Longview, Washington, is roughly halfway between the mouth of the Willamette River, near present-day Portland, and the mouth of the Columbia. At this point, the tawny desert country of the Columbia Gorge has given way to the forest green of the heavily wooded coastal hills. *Bill Yenne*

The U.S. Highway 101 bridge across the mouth of the Columbia at Astoria is located at the point where Clark noted in his journal that he could hear "the roreing or noise made by the waves brakeing on the rockey Shoress" of the Pacific Ocean in the distance. *Bill Yenne*

Looking across the Columbia River from this marker in Astoria, we can see Gray's Point, where the Corps of Discovery made its first camp in the vicinity of the mouth of the Columbia in November 1805. This point is slightly upstream from the U.S. Highway 101 bridge. *Bill Yenne*

After they came ashore, Lewis and Clark traveled west through what is now Ilwaco, Washington. U.S. Highway 101 turns north in the direction that William Clark explored between November 11 and November 18, 1805. State Route 100 takes modern travelers to Cape Disappointment, where the Corps had its first unobstructed view of the Pacific. *Bill Yenne*

A simple sign on this building identifies Astoria as the "End of the Trail." It's not quite the end, but barring traffic, one could almost drive there from here before one's ice cream cone melted. *Bill Yenne*

They imagined that the "Ocian" would be—as the term "pacific" implies—peaceful. It was certainly not. Clark confided in his journal that the ocean was "tempestuous and horrible." Clark took to referring to it as the "Great Western Ocian," adding the tongue-and-cheek comment that "I cant Say Pasific as Since I have Seen it, it has been the reverse."

By November 17, Lewis finally succeeded in reaching Captain John Meares' Cape Disappointment in the company of some Chinook men. A half-century later, the bluff where the captain had his first unobstructed view of the "Great Western Ocian" became home to a beacon to guide ships across the treacherous bar. The Cape Disappointment Lighthouse began operating in 1856. Over the years, this stretch of barely navigable seaway earned the grim nickname "Graveyard of the Pacific."

In 1862, the U.S. Army established Fort Canby on Cape Disappointment, and gun emplacements were constructed on the adjacent bluff to guard the mouth of the Columbia. After World War II, the Army turned the facility over to the state of Washington, and it became Fort Canby State Park. In time for the Lewis and Clark Bicentennial, the name was changed to the Cape Disappointment State Park. In the meantime, a Lewis and Clark Interpretive

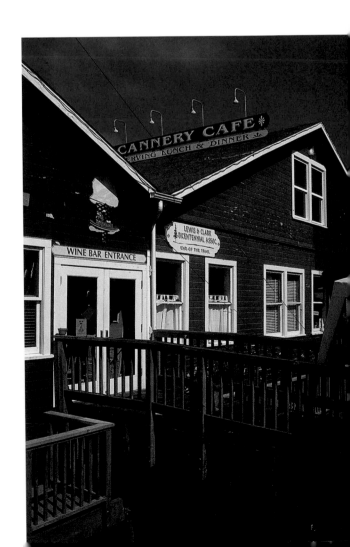

Center was opened at the park in 1975. An enclosed viewing room, 200 feet above the waves, offers a spectacular panoramic view and exhibits describing the Lewis and Clark expedition and the 19 days the Corps of Discovery spent in Pacific County, Washington.

The parking lot at the base of the bluff at Cape Disappointment marks Milepost 3,574 on the odometer from Camp Dubois. Here, the expedition had arrived at its most western point.

It was now generally understood that the Corps would have to spend the winter near the mouth of the Columbia, and it was becoming urgent to find a better campsite.

Across the Columbia River from Astoria, and a short distance downstream from the bridge, U.S. Highway 101 passes Chinook Point. Although the weather was good when this picture was taken, this is the place where winter storms caused the Corps of Discovery to halt its downstream trek by canoe and go ashore. The open ocean can be seen straight ahead, due west from Chinook Point. *Bill Yenne*

The end of the trail at last. The Washington State Lewis and Clark Interpretive Center was constructed atop the bluff at Cape Disappointment in 1975. *Donella Lucero, Washington State Parks*

The Lewis and Clark trail passes through 11 states from Camp Dubois to Cape Disappointment, with a myriad of roads marked with the official sign. This one on U.S. Highway 101, near Ilwaco, Washington, is the last sign before Cape Disappointment. Because Lewis and Clark were ashore by this point in 1805, the highway closely follows their probable actual trail. *Bill Yenne*

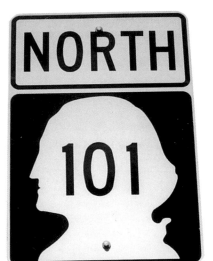

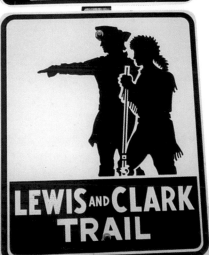

The Cape Disappointment Lighthouse is pictured here as viewed from the Lewis and Clark Interpretive Center. It has been in service since 1856, and on the bicentennial of the captains' visit, it stood as the oldest lighthouse still in use on the West Coast. *Bill Yenne*

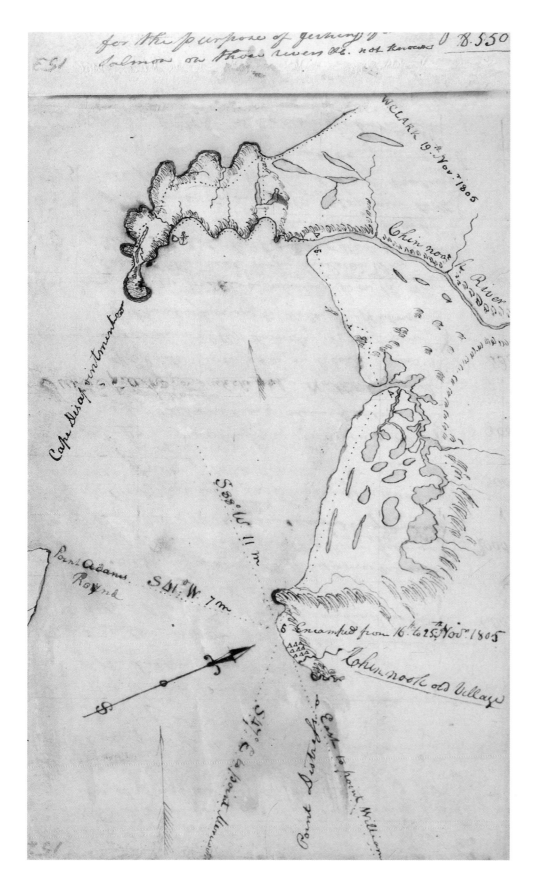

This map from the journals of
Lewis and Clark shows the mouth
of the Columbia River and Cape
Disappointment and traces the
activities of the Corps of Discovery
between November 16 and 25, 1805.
Courtesy American Philosophical Society

Chapter Ten

Cold and Rainy, Every Day

On November 18, 1805, William Clark set out with 11 men to hike overland to Cape Disappointment and scout out the coast farther north for a couple of days toward the modern resort town of Long Beach. When Clark returned to Baker Bay on November 20, it was decided to explore the southern—now Oregon—side of the mouth of the Columbia as well. Because it was impossible to cross the mouth of the Columbia, where 200-foot cedar logs and other flotsam in the surging waves were a danger to their canoes, they worked their way back upstream to cross.

This dramatic 1905 painting by Charles Marion Russell shows the Corps of Discovery meeting the Chinook people, with their intricately decorated canoes, near the mouth of the Columbia. The canoe in the foreground is the one that Clark had proudly acquired from the Wishram people. He is seen standing next to Sacagawea, who is communicating with the Chinook leader through sign language. Both York and Charbonneau are also in this canoe. The painting, *Lewis and Clark on the Lower Columbia*, is an opaque and transparent watercolor over a graphite underdrawing on paper. It's part of a collection at the Amon Carter Museum in Fort Worth, Texas. *Courtesy Amon Carter*

On December 5, Lewis finally located a suitable winter campsite amid the bogs and bays, a short distance up what they called the Netul River, a few miles southwest of Astoria. They began cutting cedars for the construction of their winter quarters two days later. Essentially finished by Christmas, the garrison was named Fort Clatsop in honor of the indigenous people who lived on the south side of the mouth of the Columbia. This followed the practice of the previous winter, when their station was named for the Mandan.

The winter of 1805–1806 was in sharp contrast with the previous winter. At Fort Mandan, they experienced snow and dramatic subzero temperatures. At Fort Clatsop, they were subjected to virtually continuous rain. Although it was never cold enough to snow, the perpetual dampness was even more bone-chilling than the blizzards of the plains.

Relations with their neighbors, the furtive Clatsop, were far more strained than those with the congenial Mandan during the previous winter. The Mandan, like the Shoshone, were mostly generous. In contrast, the people of the Pacific Coast were generally indifferent to the strangers, and there were incidents of reported thievery. The journals contain a great deal of griping. The Corps traded with the locals for skins and wapato roots, a tuber similar to the potato, but complained that they "asked enormous prices." The native people preferred blue trade beads, and most would not accept the red ones.

Food was another constant source of grumbling. On the plains, they had more to eat. At Fort Clatsop, they hunted for elk, but the few they found had little meat on their bones, and the climate caused the meat to spoil. Drouillard set out traps and managed to catch some otters.

Their Christmas dinner consisted of fish and elk meat that seemed to have gone bad. From the Tillamook people, who lived farther to the south, they were introduced to whale blubber, which Lewis thought tasted like dog or beaver.

The choice of where to build winter quarters was put to a vote in December 1805. This roadside marker at Chinook Point, Washington, discusses this decision-making process that was unique because a black man (York) and an Indian woman (Sacagawea) cast votes. This was at a time when neither of those demographics was permitted to vote in the United States. Of course, in 1805, neither Washington nor Oregon existed as part of the United States. *Bill Yenne*

The 1805–1806 winter quarters for the Corps of Discovery were located several miles south of the mouth of the Columbia and was known as Fort Clatsop. The foundations for the rooms at Fort Clatsop were completed by December 10, 1805, and the walls were finished four days later. The roof was finished on Christmas Eve. This replica was completed in 1955 at the best-guess location of the original site. *Bill Yenne*

The parade ground at Fort Clatsop had a gate at either end that was locked at night. As seen here, the smaller of the two gates was used to reach the spring. On the right is a replica of the sentinel box that was built on the last day of 1805. *Bill Yenne*

On the first day of 1806, Lewis observed that "Our repast of this day tho better than that of Christmass, consisted principally in the anticipation of the 1st day of January 1807, when in the bosom of our friends we hope to participate in the mirth and hilarity of the day, and when with the zest given by the recollection of the present, we shall completely, both mentally and corporally, enjoy the repast which the hand of civilization has prepared for us."

One of the accoutrements of "civilization" the Corps craved was salt. Not only did salt improve the flavor of the sparse rations they were eating, it was also useful in preserving meat. Within a week of their moving into their winter quarters, it was decided that their major project for the remainder of their winter at Fort Clatsop would be salt-making. There was a vast ocean filled with salt just four miles away, and it could be extracted from the seawater by boiling. In addition to its use by the Corps, salt was a valuable trade commodity as they returned back across the continent in the spring.

On January 3, a hunting party reported that they had located an ideal place for a salt-making camp near a bay 15 miles to the south, within the present town of Seaside, Oregon. There were encampments of unusually friendly Clatsop and Tillamook people nearby, and hunting seemed to be good in the area. Using five brass "kittles," a salt-making team that consisted of William Bratton, Joseph Field, and George Gibson began boiling seawater and extracting salt at a rate of up to a gallon a day. A month of work netted a bushel of salt, but over the ensuing three weeks, the team seemed to have developed more momentum. By the time they closed up shop on February 20, the men had produced more than three bushels.

While the Corpsmen distilled salt, gathered meat, and tanned hides to make footwear for the long trip home, Sacagawea's son, Jean Baptiste, had his first birthday in February, and the captains sat down to work on their journals and reflect on the more than 4,000 river miles and 18 months that had brought them to this place.

Today, the Fort Clatsop National Monument parking lot marks Milepost 3,594 on the odometer from Camp Dubois. The Salt Works at Seaside stands at Milepost 3,611. The route of the 18-month trek can now be driven in two weeks or less, but not much less.

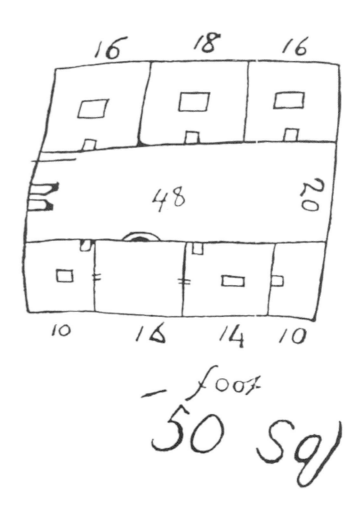

Although written descriptions of Fort Clatsop in the expedition journals are vague, both William Clark and Sergeant John Ordway sketched floor plans. This one by Clark provides the interior dimensions of the 2,500-square-foot facility. The fort consisted of two parallel buildings divided into individual rooms, and flanked a central parade ground. The side with three rooms contained the enlisted men's quarters. The four rooms on the opposite side included the room shared by Lewis and Clark, one that was used by Sacagawea and her family, an orderly room, and a storeroom. *National Park Service*

Essentially, this is the end of the Lewis and Clark trail. From the canoe landing at the base of the low hill where the fort was constructed, the Corps was no longer outbound into the unknown, but rather on the road home.

March 23, 1806, dawned "raney and uncertain." The rain should not have been equated with uncertainty, for rain had been observed by the Corps as a virtual certainty. In their entire stay at the mouth of the Columbia, the better part of five months, only 12 days had been without rain. What made March 23 different was that this was the day earmarked by the captains as the date of their departure from Fort Clatsop. Hunting parties had been dispatched for several days to acquire a final supply of meat, and the "baggage" had been packed. The only uncertainty was whether the present storm was enough delay departure for another night.

They had planned to stay longer at Fort Clatsop, not wanting to attempt crossing the Rockies before early June, but the men were fed up and itching to get moving. Everyone was anxious to get home to what the captains referred to as the "U'States."

The fort the Corps of Discovery had moved into on Christmas Eve in 1805 was abandoned by them two days short of three months later. They gave it to a Clatsop chief named Coboway, who was "more hospitable" to the Corps than were others of his nation. He may have used it for a while, but it was eventually reclaimed by nature in the damp Northwest climate. In the meantime, it was visited and used by later travelers. Gabriel Franchere, who arrived with John Jacob Astor's Pacific Fur Company in 1811, five years after Lewis and Clark departed, visited the site and recorded having seen the logs of Fort Clatsop.

In 1813, Alexander Henry of the North West Company wrote that he'd seen 25 foot trees growing among the ruins. In the early 1820s, a man named Townsend found a couple

The enlisted men's barracks at Fort Clatsop were finished on Christmas Eve and had bunk beds and wooden floors. Fireplaces were added after Christmas. The elk antlers are consistent with what one might have seen in a similar room at the original fort. *Bill Yenne*

The bunks in the quarters used by Lewis and Clark at Fort Clatsop were similar to those they shared a year earlier at Fort Mandan. A coonskin cap is seen on the wall next to the three-cornered hat that was standard U.S. Army issue. *Bill Yenne*

The chimneys at the original Fort Clatsop were probably completed during the first week of 1806. The replica chimneys topped off the structure in August 1955. *Bill Yenne*

For the construction of the Fort Clatsop replica, the Crown Zellerbach company donated 408 logs, and each were roughly 10 feet long with a minimum diameter of 7 inches. They came from the company's timber holdings near Vernonia, Oregon, and were pulled out of the woods using draft horses in order to avert any scarring by modern logging equipment. They were then treated to preserve them in the damp climate that eventually destroyed the original fort. *Bill Yenne*

of peace medals in the vicinity. Beginning around 1850, a succession of settlers cleared the land and set about farming, and later in the century, logging and pottery businesses operated at or near the site. The location of the site and a description of the fort was passed through several generations of local people and was still fairly well known until the late nineteenth century.

However, by the time the Oregon Historical Society acquired the site in 1901, no trace of the original fort could be found, and the exact location was uncertain. Carlos Shane, the first resident settler of the site in the 1850s, was still alive, and he claimed to remember the location. What makes his recollection plausible is that he described what the ruins looked like. He said the fort consisted of two parallel structures about 30 feet long and 15 feet apart, a description that matches that in the sketch in Clark's journal. This is important because Clark's sketch wasn't published until 1904. Until then there was no way he could know the size and layout of the fort without actually having seen it.

In 1955, a replica was reconstructed in the general vicinity of where Shane remembered Fort Clatsop had been. The replica was based on the detailed floor plan that Clark drew.

The entrance to the Fort Clatsop National Memorial is shown here as it appeared at the time of the bicentennial. After the federal government acquired the site in 1958, the road leading to the location from U.S. Highway 101 was paved. *Bill Yenne*

Three years later, the National Park Service took over management of the site, including the replica fort, as the Fort Clatsop National Memorial. In an effort to find the elusive true location once and for all, several archaeological studies were undertaken between 1961 and 1996, but the success enjoyed by Dan Hall at Travelers' Rest had still eluded the archaeologists at Fort Clatsop at the time of the bicentennial.

Today, the replica is furnished with hand-hewn wooden bunks, tables, benches, and chairs, and staffed by knowledgeable interpretive personnel. It serves as an "outdoor museum that makes history fun for over 200,000 visitors a year, providing real life, hands-on experiences." One can visit the fort and walk to what was likely the Lewis and Clark canoe landing on what the captains called the Netul River, but which is now the Lewis and Clark River.

Meanwhile, in 1900, the Oregon Historical Society had also identified the possible, if not probable, location of the Salt Works at Seaside. They interviewed Jenny Michel, a Clatsop woman born in 1816, who related her father's recollection of white men boiling water on the beach. Some soot-blackened rocks at the place she identified were donated to the state of Oregon in 1910 by the landowner, Charlotte Moffett Cartwright, from the estate of Charles Morrison Cartwright. The area was fenced off, and a plaque was installed at the time of the Lewis and Clark Sesquicentennial in 1955 by the Seaside Lion's Club, who managed the site. Through the years, the Oregon Historical Society offered to donate the site to the National Park Service, but the latter expressed doubts about the archeological authenticity of the site. In 1978, it finally become a detached section of Fort Clatsop National Memorial.

Today you can relive the experience of Fort Clatsop in miniature with this 153-piece kit from Lincoln Logs. Fog and drizzle not included. *Bill Yenne*

The visitor center at the Fort Clatsop National Memorial was opened in 1963. The annual number of visitors reached a million in 1991, and in 2004, the parking lot at the visitor center was closed in favor of using shuttle buses to bring people in from satellite parking lots. *Bill Yenne*

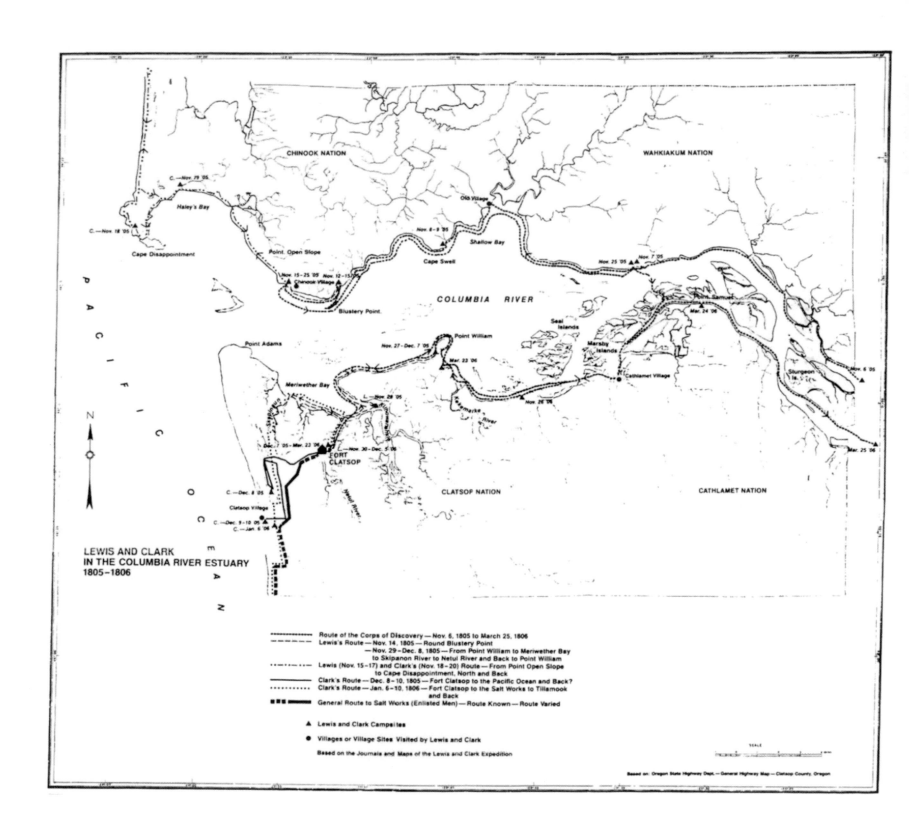

LEWIS AND CLARK
IN THE COLUMBIA RIVER ESTUARY
1805–1806

.... Route of the Corps of Discovery — Nov. 6, 1805 to March 25, 1806
— — — Lewis's Route — Nov. 14, 1805 — Round Blustery Point
        — Nov. 29–Dec. 8, 1805 — From Point William to Meriwether Bay
        to Skipanon River to Netul River and Back to Point William
—·—·— Lewis (Nov. 15–17) and Clark's (Nov. 18–20) Route — From Point Open Slope
        to Cape Disappointment, North and Back
———— Clark's Route — Dec. 8–10, 1805 — Fort Clatsop to the Pacific Ocean and Back?
············ Clark's Route — Jan. 6–10, 1806 — Fort Clatsop to the Salt Works to Tillamook
        and Back
▪▪▪▬▬▬ General Route to Salt Works (Enlisted Men) — Route Known — Route Varied

▲ Lewis and Clark Campsites

● Villages or Village Sites Visited by Lewis and Clark

Based on the Journals and Maps of the Lewis and Clark Expedition

Based on: Oregon State Highway Dept. — General Highway Map — Clatsop County, Oregon

This map shows the mouth of the Columbia River and the location of Fort Clatsop. Also indicated are various trips taken by members of the Corps of Discovery during the winter of 1805–1806. *National Park Service*

Above: This replica of a cottonwood dugout canoe is on display a short distance from the replica of Fort Clatsop. It is also near the place on the Lewis and Clark River (then known as the Netul River) where the Corps of Discovery landed and stored their canoes through the winter of 1805–1806. *Bill Yenne*

Above: This spot on the Lewis and Clark River is a likely candidate for being the canoe landing used by the Corps of Discovery. The vertical posts, seen in the background, are the remnants of docks built during logging operations in the area. A sawmill owned by Richard Moore existed near here from 1852 to 1854, and lumber produced at the mill was shipped to San Francisco. The Oregon Steam Navigation Company later operated in this section of the river. *Bill Yenne*

Left: This sign on the oceanfront Promenade in Seaside, Oregon, points to the supposed site of the salt works. If the site is correct, salt-makers William Bratton, Joseph Field, and George Gibson would have lugged their "kittles" of seawater along this trail. The Pacific Ocean is visible in the distance. *Bill Yenne*

of small fish which now begin to run and are
taken in great quantities in the Columbia R.
about 40 miles above us by means of skiming
or scooping nets. on this page I have drawn
the likeness of them as large as life; it
as perfect as I can make it with my
pen and will serve to give a
general idea of the fish. the
rays of the fins are boney but
not sharp tho' somewhat pointed.
the small fin on the back
next to the tail has no
rays of bone being a
brearans pellicle.
to the gills have
each. those of the
ight each, those
re 20 and a
'at of the back
he fins are of
s of a bleuish
ta the lower
s of a silve=
art. the
chid the
cecond of
a
a pruple
silver
ed

thin mem.
the fins next
eleven rays
abdomen have
of the pinnaani
half formed in front.
has eleven rays. all
a white colour. the back
duskey colour and that of
part of the sides and belly
ong white. no spots on any
first bone of the gills next
eye is of a bleuis cast, and the
a light gaald colour nearly white.
of the eye is black and the iris of
white. the under jaw exceeds the uper;
the mouth opens to great extent, folding,
that of the herring. it has no teeth.
the abdomen is obtuse and smooth; in this
differing from the herring, shad anchovey;
8c of the Malacapterygious Order & Class
Clupea

The fence around the salt cairn area was built as early as 1900, and this permanent plaque was installed during the Lewis and Clark sesquicentennial in 1955. *Bill Yenne*

Shown here is Tillimook Head, as viewed from the dunes west of the salt works in Seaside. Clark climbed it in early January 1806, and it is one of several places that was given the designation of "Clark's Point of View." The view of the Pacific from here would have been grand then, and it still is. *Bill Yenne*

Here is the author on the Promenade in Seaside, with the Pacific Ocean in the background, at the end of a 3,611-mile bicentennial drive from Camp Dubois. Note the Missouri license plate and the Dakota insects encrusted on the vehicle's bumper. *Mark McPike*

A short distance inland from the shoreline on the Oregon coast, the woods are a veritable jungle of thick underbrush and swamps of standing water. This made the 15-mile trek from Fort Clatsop to the salt works difficult, unless one could find and use one of the trails used by the Clatsop or Tillimook people. *Bill Yenne*

Members of the Corps, often led by William Clark, made several trips along the Oregon coast, south of the salt works, into the area populated by the Tillamook people. In January 1806, when the Tillamook people reported that an enormous whale had come ashore on a beach similar to this one, Clark led a party to view it and obtain some blubber to eat. Sacagawea insisted on going along to see the "monstrous fish." *Bill Yenne*

"It is with pleasure that I announce to you the safe arrival of myself and party at 12 OClk. today at this place with our papers and baggage. In obedience to your orders we have penetrated the Continent of North America to the Pacific Ocean, and sufficiently explored

posed across the continent; of this distance 200 miles is along a good road, and 140 over tremendious mountains which for 60 ms are covered with eternal snows; however a passage over these mountains is practicable from the latter part of June to the last of September, and the cheap rate at which horses are to be obtained from the Indians of the Rocky Mountains and West of them, reduces the expences of transportation over this portage to a mere trifle. The navigation of the Kooskooske, the South East branch of the

Chapter Eleven

The Long Trip Home

At 1:00 p.m. on March 23, 1806, the Corps of Discovery "bid a final adieu to Fort Clatsop" a week earlier than they had originally planned. They were anxious to get moving and get away from the damp coastal weather. They passed the mouth of the Netul (now Lewis and Clark) River and entered Meriwether's Bay—now known as Young's Bay—over which Astoria was built. Here, they passed a group of Chinook whom they knew and declined their offer to buy another canoe. At 7:00 p.m., at the mouth of a creek east of Astoria, they rendezvoused with Drouillard and a hunting party and added two elk to their larder. That night, they camped beyond the sound of the "Great Western Ocian." They were on their way home to the "U'States."

From Traveler's Rest, Meriwether Lewis crossed the Clark Fork and made his way east along the north bank of that river and passed through the site of the present city of Missoula, Montana. In this view from the north side of the Clark Fork, one can see the *M* of the University of Montana on Mount Sentinel. Rattlesnake Creek enters on the left, and Hellgate Canyon is upstream. *Bill Yenne*

The return to St. Louis took six months, compared to the 18 months spent on the outbound leg. The principal reason for this was that the majority of the distance both ways was on the Missouri River, and on the return, they traveled with the current, not against it. Two other essential reasons were that they weren't exploring new territory, but following a route that they knew, and perhaps most important of all, they were going home!

In 1805, it had taken 20 days from when they entered the Columbia until Clark noted that the "ocian" was in view. In 1806, traveling against the current of the Columbia, it took them 36 days to reach the mouth of the Walla Walla River, about 10 river miles downstream from the mouth of the Snake River at Pasco, Washington. It was from here that they headed out across the open plains instead of following the Snake River. On the return, they traded for horses at the Dalles and used them to carry their baggage along the north side of the Columbia River Gorge.

At the mouth of the Walla Walla, Chief Yellept (a.k.a. Yellepet) of the Walla Walla people informed Lewis that "there was a good road which passed from the Columbia opposite to this village to the entrance of the Kooskooske [Clearwater River]." With Yellept, Clark traded his sword for an "eligant white horse."

Two weeks after leaving Fort Clatsop, the Corps of Discovery reached the point where Meriwether Lewis wrote that they were beyond the tidal influence of the Pacific Ocean. The actual Rooster Rock was called Beacon Rock by Lewis and Clark. Oregon's Rooster Rock State Park is 170 highway miles from Fort Clatsop. *Bill Yenne*

This road, now known locally as "The Forgotten Trail," follows the general route of Washington State Route 124 and U.S. Highway 12 through the towns of Prescott, Waitsburg, Dayton, and Pomeroy. Although it was shorter in distance than the route taken on the Snake River in 1805, the overland trek took about two weeks as opposed to the 10 days in 1804. Of course, had they returned via the river, they would have been going upstream, and it may have taken at least two weeks to reach the mouth of the Clearwater.

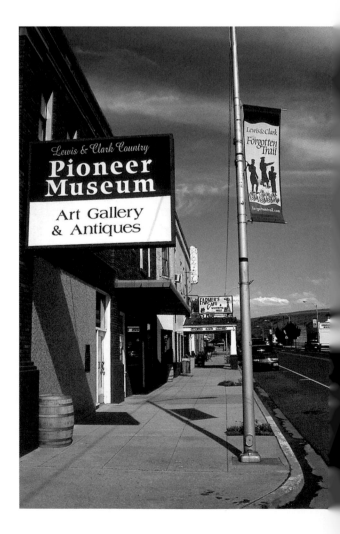

In 1806, the Corps of Discovery followed the Columbia upstream, but instead of continuing east by following their 1805 route on the Snake River, they decided to travel over land. Today this route is remembered as the "Forgotten Trail" because descriptions of this part of the trek of Lewis and Clark are typically glossed over in accounts of the trip. *Bill Yenne*

On May 7, as they followed the Clearwater east toward the mountains, the Corps met the Nez Perce and were reunited with their old friend, Chief Twisted Hair, who had cared for their horses over the winter. A week later, they were back to Weippe Prairie, where they had first met the Nez Perce eight months earlier. Here they learned there was still considerable snow on Lolo Pass, so they decided to wait there for a few weeks.

The Castlemoyle bookshop in Pomeroy, Washington, gives travelers a unique opportunity to join the Corps of Discovery along the Forgotten Trail. *Bill Yenne*

"At the distance of fifteen miles from the river and on the Eastern border of this plain the Rocky Mountains commence and present us with winter at it's utmost extreem," Lewis observed. "The snow is yet many feet deep even near the base of these mountains; here we have summer spring and winter within the short space of 15 or 20 miles."

Their time waiting for spring to reach the high country was spent hunting for elk and other game. Memories of nearly starving on this leg of the trip in 1805 were still fresh in the minds of the members of the expedition.

Finally, it was time to go. On June 15, Lewis and Clark started eastward across the Bitterroots accompanied by several Nez Perce. The Corps' 66 horses included those acquired from the Walla Walla, as well as those the Nez Perce had boarded through the winter. On June 29, they were basking in the warm waters of Lolo Hot Springs, and by sundown the next day, they were back at Travelers' Rest.

The previous year, they arrived at Travelers' Rest on September 9, after they departed the Great Falls on July 15, nearly two months earlier. While at Travelers' Rest, the captains had been told by the Salish that there was an alternate overland route that could get them to the Great Falls in four days. The Nez Perce confirmed this story.

As they planned their return during their long weeks at Fort Clatsop, the captains had decided that they would split up at Travelers' Rest and cross the entire breadth of Montana separately. Lewis took the four-day trail to the Great Falls, while Clark returned south and ascended the Bitterroot River, crossed the Continental Divide, and retrieved their cache at Camp Fortunate. These two parties were then further subdivided. Lewis left men at the Falls and made a reconnaissance to the north. Clark divided his group at the Three Forks of the Missouri. One contingent went north to the Falls to meet the men from Lewis' command waiting there, while Clark himself crossed the mountains in search of the Yellowstone River.

The Forgotten Trail even has its Forgotten Three Forks, albeit less geographically important than Montana's Three Forks. Mainly, the Corps followed Pataha Creek, but they also crossed Patit Creek and the Tucannon River and named the latter "Lewis' River." *Bill Yenne*

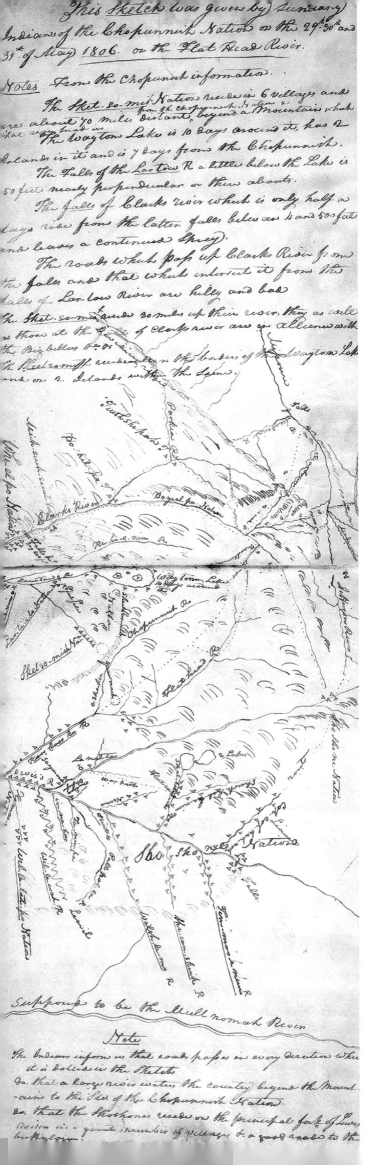

The Lewis and Clark Cafe in Lolo, Montana, is less than a mile from Traveler's Rest, where the Corps of Discovery camped on two memorable occasions. Lolo is at the intersection of U.S. Highways 12 and 93 in a place that had been a crossroads of major Indian trails for more than a century when the captains passed this way. In 1806, Lewis and Clark parted company here and didn't cross one another's path for more than a thousand miles. *Bill Yenne*

When Lewis met the other two groups at the Great Falls, they traveled downstream on the Missouri to rendezvous with Clark near the mouth of the Yellowstone.

The captains split up on July 3. That evening, Lewis reached what is now known as the Clark Fork River, a misnomer because it was Lewis, not Clark, who came this way. The following day, Lewis, George Drouillard, Sergeant Gass, and seven privates conducted the first Fourth of July military parade through what is now downtown Missoula. They crossed Rattlesnake Creek, headed through the canyon that would be known as Hellgate, and reached the mouth of the Blackfoot River near the present town of Bonner.

Next, using the well-marked trail used by many tribes, they turned east to follow the Blackfoot River toward the mountains. This route is now generally followed by Montana State Route 200. Three days later, they crossed the Continental Divide near Lewis and Clark Pass—another misnomer, because Clark never saw it.

On July 11, Lewis and his party reached the upstream side of the Great Falls of the Missouri and recognized the place where they'd camped 12 months earlier. It had taken them a week, rather than four days, from Missoula, but that was far better than two months! They went hunting, and Lewis spotted a herd of buffalo that he estimated at 10,000. The men ate very well and were delighted to no longer depend on scrawny elk and spoiling fish.

Lewis set out on his northern reconnaissance with Drouillard, Joseph and Reubin Fields, and a half dozen horses, and left Sergeant Patrick Gass, with most of the men, to dig up the

Among the maps contained within the Lewis and Clark journals, this one, sketched in late May 1806, is among the most significant. It shows a detailed overview of the headwaters of the Snake and Missouri rivers and their connections. Considering what they had to work with, the captains did a remarkable job. *Courtesy American Philosophical Society*

caches left the previous year and to wait for Clark's contingent. The purpose of Lewis' mission was to scout the upper reaches of Maria's River. Because it was calculated to be the major northern tributary of the Missouri, it defined the northern extent of the Missouri River drainage and the northern boundary of the Louisiana Purchase.

Jefferson hoped that this boundary could be determined to be north of 50 degrees, thus pushing north the border between the United States and the British territory that would become part of Canada. It was a purely economic issue. The more territory that could be diverted to the United States by this geographic feature, the more of the potentially lucrative fur trade that could be diverted to Americans.

On July 21, Lewis and the others reached the mouth of what Lewis called the north branch of Maria's River, now known as Cut Bank Creek. By the following day, they had reached the northernmost bend of this creek and made camp within sight of the jagged mountains of today's Glacier National Park. The weather was overcast, and Lewis wanted to wait for clear weather to take a sextant reading to confirm their latitude. Lewis wrote that he had "lost all hope of the waters of this river ever extending to N Latitude 50 degrees." He was right; it is just north of 48 degrees. They called their encampment "Camp Disappointment" in honor of this setback to Jefferson's dreams of a slightly larger America.

In the two centuries that followed, the site has changed little. As with many sections of the Lewis and Clark trail, it is still extremely remote and located on private rangeland within the Blackfeet Reservation. No paved road is nearby, but it is possible to walk to it, if one inquires ahead of time at the privately owned Meriwether Meadows Campground. Located two miles north of U.S. Highway 2 on State Route 444, Meriwether Meadows affords the opportunity to camp within three miles of the northernmost encampment of the Lewis and Clark expedition.

Lewis and the men broke camp on July 26 to head back to the Missouri. They had ridden about 20 miles and had crossed the Two Medicine River

A few hours after passing through what would become Missoula, Meriwether Lewis and his party reached the site of the present lumber town of Bonner, at the mouth of the Blackfoot River. In 2002, this Jim Rogers sculpture of Lewis and Seaman was erected in Bonner to commemorate Independence Day 1806. *Bill Yenne*

As they followed the Blackfoot River upstream, Lewis and the others traveled on a trail that had been used for many years by tribes, such as the Nez Perce, who crossed the Rocky Mountains to hunt buffalo on the plains. Today, Montana State Route 200 follows this trail. *Bill Yenne*

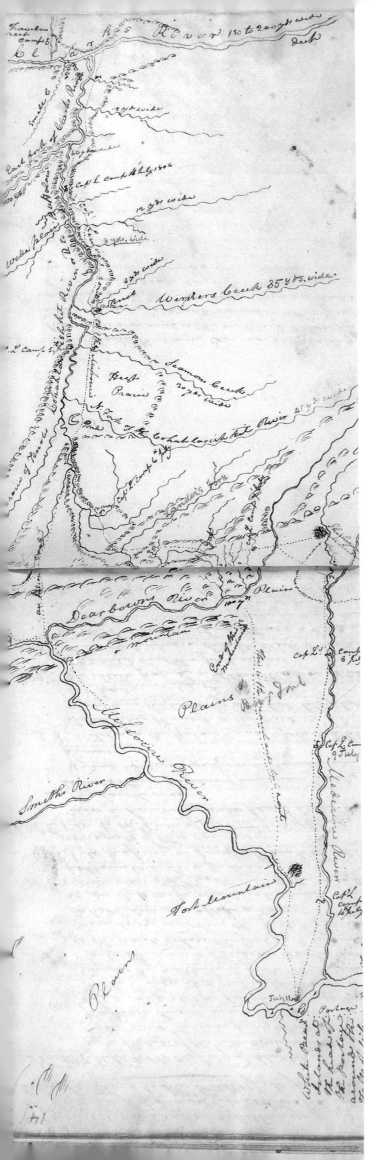

This map, drawn by Meriwether Lewis, traced his route from Travelers' Rest to the Missouri River between July 3 and 11, 1806. *American Philosophical Society*

when they came over a rise and saw a large number of horses and eight riders. This was the first encounter of the Corps of Discovery with the Blackfeet, or Siksika, and it would not be a pleasant one. The Shoshone, Salish, and Nez Perce, who were in a constant state of war with the Blackfeet, warned Lewis and Clark about their mortal enemies, so Lewis was wary of these men. Unlike the other tribes that Lewis and Clark had encountered on the plains, they were armed with guns they received in trade from the British.

At the suggestion of the eight men, who turned out to be Piegan, one of three major divisions of the Blackfeet, they all camped together for the night. A pipe was passed, and Lewis presented a Jefferson peace medal and other token gifts. Lewis explained that he had made peace with the other tribes and hoped to imply that he now wanted to make peace between the Blackfeet and the U.S. government.

It has been suggested that the Piegan became angry when they interpreted Lewis as having said that he had allied the other tribes against the Blackfeet, but nobody will ever know for certain. In any case, shortly before dawn, the Piegan attempted to steal the men's rifles. In the ensuing scuffle, the rifles were recovered, but Reubin Fields killed one of the Piegans with a knife. Meanwhile, other Piegans attempted to steal the horses. One of them shot at Lewis, and he returned fire. Lewis hit the shooter, and the rest of the Piegan fled.

The Piegan had moved to a large encampment of their tribe nearby, so it was a foregone conclusion that a large number of warriors would be returning soon. The four members of the Corps mounted up and headed toward the Missouri River at top speed. Lewis estimated that they rode 63 miles before they rested and another 37 miles before they made camp. By now it was past midnight, and they traveled by the light of the moon.

The Two Medicine "fight site," a dozen miles south of Cut Bank, Montana, is still enigmatic because it is located on private land and not open to the public. Out here, the penalty for trespassing is the same as what Lewis meted out for horse stealing two centuries ago. The West is still a place apart. The West is still wild.

While Lewis went north toward Camp Disappointment, Clark traveled south. By the time Lewis crossed the Continental Divide at Lewis and Clark Pass, Clark had reached the vicinity of Lost Trail Pass and crossed the divide. Rather than pushing south along the Salmon River to Lemhi Pass, Clark chose to turn east and cross at what is now Joseph Pass. It was named for the Nez Perce chief, whose 1877 running battle with the U.S. Army became one of the legendary epics of the nineteenth century. Clark passed through the vast valley of the Big Hole, near the battlefield of the same name where Chief Joseph's warriors won an important victory in the 1877 war.

Proceeding eastward across Big Hole Pass, Clark's party was again within the watershed of the Missouri River headwaters. On July 8, they reached Camp Fortunate. The canoes and cached supplies were recovered, and on July 10, they were underway and returned down

This monument, located near U.S. Highway 2 on the Blackfeet Reservation, just east of Browning, Montana, commemorates Lewis' northward trek to Camp Disappointment. It is visible from the rails traveled by the *Empire Builder* passenger train, a creation of the Great Northern Railway that is now operated by Amtrak. The monument is several miles from Camp Disappointment. *Bill Yenne*

IS IT BLACKFEET OR BLACKFOOT?

———◆———

The correct term for the Algonquian-speaking American Indian tribe is *Blackfeet*, although they are known in their own language as Siksika (pronounced as "sheek-sheek-awah"). The term *Blackfoot* has been attached to numerous geographical features in the West, including the river that Lewis traveled and a glacier in Glacier National Park. The Blackfeet people consist of three major branches, the Blood, the Piegan, and the Blackfeet proper.

Overcast weather also greeted Meriwether Lewis when he camped here in July 1806. The small enclosure on the island in Cut Bank Creek marks the probable location of Camp Disappointment. The Rocky Mountains within Glacier National Park are visible in the distance. *Bill Yenne*

The Bitterroot Range can be seen in the distance from an old corral in Montana's Big Hole Valley. In July 1806, William Clark traveled through this broad valley. When he left Travelers' Rest with Sacagawea and the others, Clark went south and crossed the mountains roughly 80 miles north of Lemhi Pass, where everyone had crossed the previous year. *Bill Yenne*

Clark and Sacagawea passed through this area. A gravel road departs from Montana State Route 278 near the top of Big Hole Pass. *Bill Yenne*

Jefferson's River, paddling their first oar strokes on the continuous run to St. Louis. Traveling with the current, the canoes reached the Three Forks of the Missouri by July 13 and kept pace with the expedition's horses ashore. At Three Forks, Sergeant John Ordway took command of the canoes for the rendezvous at the Great Falls with Lewis, while Clark took the horses and headed east toward the Yellowstone.

Ordway and the canoes arrived at the Great Falls on July 26. As luck would have it, they had finished portaging their canoes two days later, just as Lewis, Drouillard, and the Fields brothers arrived there from their epic overland dash from the Two Medicine River. Under the presumption that a Piegan war party was hot on his heels, Lewis lost no time. The horses were stripped of baggage and released, the canoes and white pirogue were packed, and the men were underway on the Missouri River. Reaching the mouth of Maria's River, they examined the red pirogue and found "her so much decayed that it was impossible with the means we had to repare her."

Two days after leaving the Great Falls, they were already in the vicinity of the Fred Robinson Bridge, and Lewis noted "the current strong and the men anxious." The year before, this stretch of the Missouri had taken them 19

Named for Clark's nickname for Sacagawea's baby, Pompey's Pillar is the highest overlook along the Yellowstone River between Billings and Miles City. It was an important site for the Crow people, who referred to it as the place "Where the Mountain Lion Preys." *Bill Yenne*

days. In 1806, Patrick Gass estimated that they made 88 miles on August 4 alone. Three days later, they were approaching the mouth of the Yellowstone.

Three weeks had now passed since Clark had left Ordway at Three Forks and had gone east in the company of York, Sergeant Nathaniel Pryor, seven privates, and the Charbonneau family. They followed the Gallatin River to the vicinity of Belgrade, Montana, continued across Bozeman Pass, and reached the Yellowstone River at the present site of Livingston on July 15.

Today, Interstate 90 follows Clark's Trail from Three Forks to Livingston, and it follows both the trail and the Yellowstone as far as Billings, Montana. At Billings, the state's oil industry boom town and largest city, Interstate 90 angles south to cross South Dakota toward Chicago and Boston. Interstate 94 is born here to carry the Interstate Highway System to Bismarck and across North Dakota, also following the Yellowstone.

On July 25, 1806, William Clark carved his name in the soft stone on the side of Pompey's Pillar. He noted in his journals that he had carved his name many places, but this is the only one that was ever found. He was not the first here at Pompey's Pillar. He noted that he saw many pictograms carved here by Native Americans. Clark's signature has been protected by glass since 1954. *Bill Yenne*

This is the view looking north across the Yellowstone River from the top of Pompey's Pillar. The scene is virtually unchanged since William Clark showed it to Pompey himself in 1806. *Bill Yenne*

Clark's party remained with their horses until July 20, at a point about 20 miles upstream from Billings. He decided that the Yellowstone was now wide enough to put part of his small contingent into the river, and he started looking for likely trees to make canoes. "I determined to have two Canoes made out of the largest of those trees and lash them together which will Cause them to be [sturdy] and fully Sufficient to take my Small party & Self with what little baggage we have down this river," he wrote, describing his idea for double-hulling his new vessel. He described the new conveyance as being "28 feet in length and about 16 or 18 inches deep and from 16 to 24 inches wide."

After some fussing over lost horses, which he thought might have been stolen, Clark detailed Sergeant Nathaniel Pryor to take a four-man team overland to the Knife River Villages with the horses, while Clark and the others traveled by boat. The plan was short-lived. Two nights after Clark headed downstream, Pryor's little command had their horses stolen by some Crow warriors, so Pryor's men also put into the river.

Shown here is an abandoned homestead in the Yellowstone River valley of eastern Montana. The remoteness and harsh climate has led to many failed ventures over the years. *Bill Yenne*

The mouth of the Yellowstone River is just east of the border between Montana and North Dakota. The Missouri River runs from left to right, while the Yellowstone enters from the opposite side. Clark's party passed here on August 3, 1806, followed by Lewis and his group four days later. *Bill Yenne*

They used a pair of circular "bullboats" that they fashioned after those they'd seen the Mandan make.

Meanwhile, on July 25, 1806, Clark reached what is certainly the signature point of his part of the expedition independent of his co-captain. About 25 miles downstream from where Billings now stands, there is what Clark called "a remarkable rock Situated in an extensive bottom on the [south] Side of the river & 250 paces from it." It is the only sandstone outcrop on the south side of the Yellowstone for miles in either direction, so it had been a landmark for indigenous people, especially the Crow, for centuries.

He described his remarkable rock as "200 [actually closer to 150] feet high and 400 paces in secumphrance and only axcessable on one Side." Clark ascended this rock, and from its top, he "Had a most extensive view in every direction." He went on to note that "The nativs have ingraved on the face of this rock the figures of animals &c," so Clark himself, "marked my name and the day of the month & year."

Clark's signature and the date remain here, just as he carved them into the sandstone on the northeast side of the hill two centuries ago. He named it "Pompey's Tower," in honor of little Jean Baptiste Charbonneau, who was almost certainly carried to its summit. Through the years it came to be known onomatopoeically as "Pompey's Pillar." It is a must-see for Lewis and Clark buffs because it contains the only surviving graffiti from the expedition. Other places where Corps members—especially Clark—are recorded to have carved their names have been searched for, but never found.

This replica of a Mandan-style bullboat is on display in the Jefferson Expansion Museum in St. Louis. Separated from Clark, and with their horses pilfered by the Crow, Sergeant Nathaniel Pryor and his men constructed a pair of bullboats and traveled more than 500 miles downstream on the Yellowstone and Missouri in two weeks. *Bill Yenne*

Built in 1947, the massive Garrison Dam created Lake Sakakawea, which, in turn, inundated the point on the Missouri River where Lewis and Clark were reunited after separately crossing Montana and part of North Dakota in less than five weeks. *Bill Yenne*

The next time that Clark's graffiti is known to have been seen was by pioneer prospector James Stuart in 1863. Captain Grant Marsh, of the steamboat *Josephine*, noted it in his log a dozen years later. The Northern Pacific Railroad placed an iron grate over the signature in 1882 to protect it from vandalism. The property was later acquired by a family named Foote, and in 1954, they replaced the grate with the present brass-and-glass covering. They opened it to the public through 1958, but it was closed until it was named a National Historic Landmark in late 1965. It was closed again in 1989, but reopened in 1992 when the Bureau of Land Management acquired the site. In 2001, it was redesignated as Pompey's Pillar National Monument. It is easily accessible from Interstate 94 using Exit 23, or from State Route 312.

On August 3, Clark's party reached the mouth of the Yellowstone, about 250 highway miles downstream from Pompey's Pillar. Today, the highways that follow the river, are Interstate 84 as far as Glendive, then State Route 16 to Sidney, and the ubiquitous State Route 200—which nips in and out of the Lewis and Clark Trail all across Montana—for a dozen miles to the North Dakota border. From here, North Dakota State Route 58 will get one back to Fort Union and North Dakota State Route 1804 (see Chapter 5).

Clark entered the Missouri River and proceeded downstream for another four days, finally making camp on August 7, where he planned to wait for the others. Lewis, meanwhile, arrived at the mouth of the Yellowstone on August 7 and had seen evidence of Clark's recent camp there. They were four days behind Clark, but they had made pretty good time on the Missouri in northern Montana.

On August 8, Pryor and his men overtook Clark, and had come all the way from near Pompey's Pillar in their bullboats. They reported that the bullboats had performed wonderfully without leaking. The only mishap was that Pryor was bitten by a wolf one night as they slept. He had, by now, nearly recovered.

Lewis and his command finally caught up with Clark on August 12, but they had just come close to arriving without Lewis himself. The day before they had seen a herd of elk and had stopped for Lewis and Pierre Cruzatte to go ashore to hunt. The two men separated and both brought down an elk. Cruzatte aimed at what he thought was an elk and fired. It was not an elk, but rather the buckskin-clad Lewis.

When the co-captains reunited the next day, Clark examined the wound and described it as "a very bad flesh wound the ball had passed through the fleshey part of his left thy below the hip bone and cut the cheek of the right buttock for 3 inches in length and the depth of the ball." Lewis would fully recover, but was unable to sit or walk for nearly two weeks.

The site of their reunion was on the shore of the Missouri River, 86 miles upstream from the Knife River Villages, at a place that is now far beneath the waves at Lake Sakakawea, the reservoir formed by Garrison Dam. It was the first time the captains had seen each other since July 3 at Travelers' Rest.

Traveling with the current and the anxious haste of people on their way home, the reunited Corps of Discovery made it all the way to Knife River on August 13. Here, they were reunited with Chief Sheheke, who agreed to accompany them to St. Louis and Washington, D.C. Sacagawea and Charbonneau, on the other hand, remained at Knife River. Clark, who had become quite attached to young Pompey, urged the family to come back to "civilization," where the young lad could grow up with the advantages of a proper education. They declined, but said that perhaps they would come south at some point in the future. They didn't come for three years.

After a last look at their old Fort Mandan, which had burned sometime in the past 16 months, they headed downstream. Their descent was like a greatly speeded-up movie of their ascent played in reverse. It had taken six months for the expedition to ascend the Missouri to Knife River. Traveling downstream, pushed by the current, they did it in less than six weeks. In 1804, a mile or two was often typical of a day's progress. In 1806, 60 miles a day was about average. They paused briefly to trade insults with some Lakota men, but they had little other contact with any of the indigenous people south of Knife River.

A month out of Knife River, they met American vessels traveling upstream and made contact with settlements ashore. On September 21, they reached St. Charles. They were the object of great interest. "The inhabitants of this village appear much delighted at our return," Clark wrote, "And seem to vie with each other in their politeness to us all." The men spent the night in real beds for the first time in more than two years.

The Corps learned that they were long since been given up for dead, although President Jefferson said he had not given up hope. One of Lewis' first acts upon the Corps of Discovery reaching St. Louis at noon on September 24 was to draft a letter to the president. He gave Jefferson an overview of the expedition that had succeeded in crossing the continent to the Pacific —and returned. The 8,000 miles that are now known as the Lewis and Clark Trail had come full circle.

The brick-lined and tree-shaded streets of St. Charles, Missouri, have changed little since the early nineteenth century, but the style of carriage using the streets has changed. This prosperous city must have presented an enormous culture shock for the Corps of Discovery as they returned to "civilization" after 28 months in the West. *Bill Yenne*

St. Louis September 23rd 1806
from the Indians of the Rocky Mountains and West of them, reduces
the expences of transportation over this portage to a mere trifle.
The navigation of the Kooskooske, the South East branch of the

Epilogue

❦

Meriwether Lewis finished his lengthy report to President Jefferson on September 24, 1806, and sent George Drouillard across the Mississippi to see that it got into the mail. By the time Jefferson received it a month later, the news of the success of the expedition had already spread throughout the "U'States."

❦

This monument to Sacagawea overlooks the Missouri River near Mobridge, South Dakota. She is thought to have been buried in an unmarked grave at the Fort Manuel trading post in South Dakota after her death at the age of 25 in December 1812. *Bill Yenne*

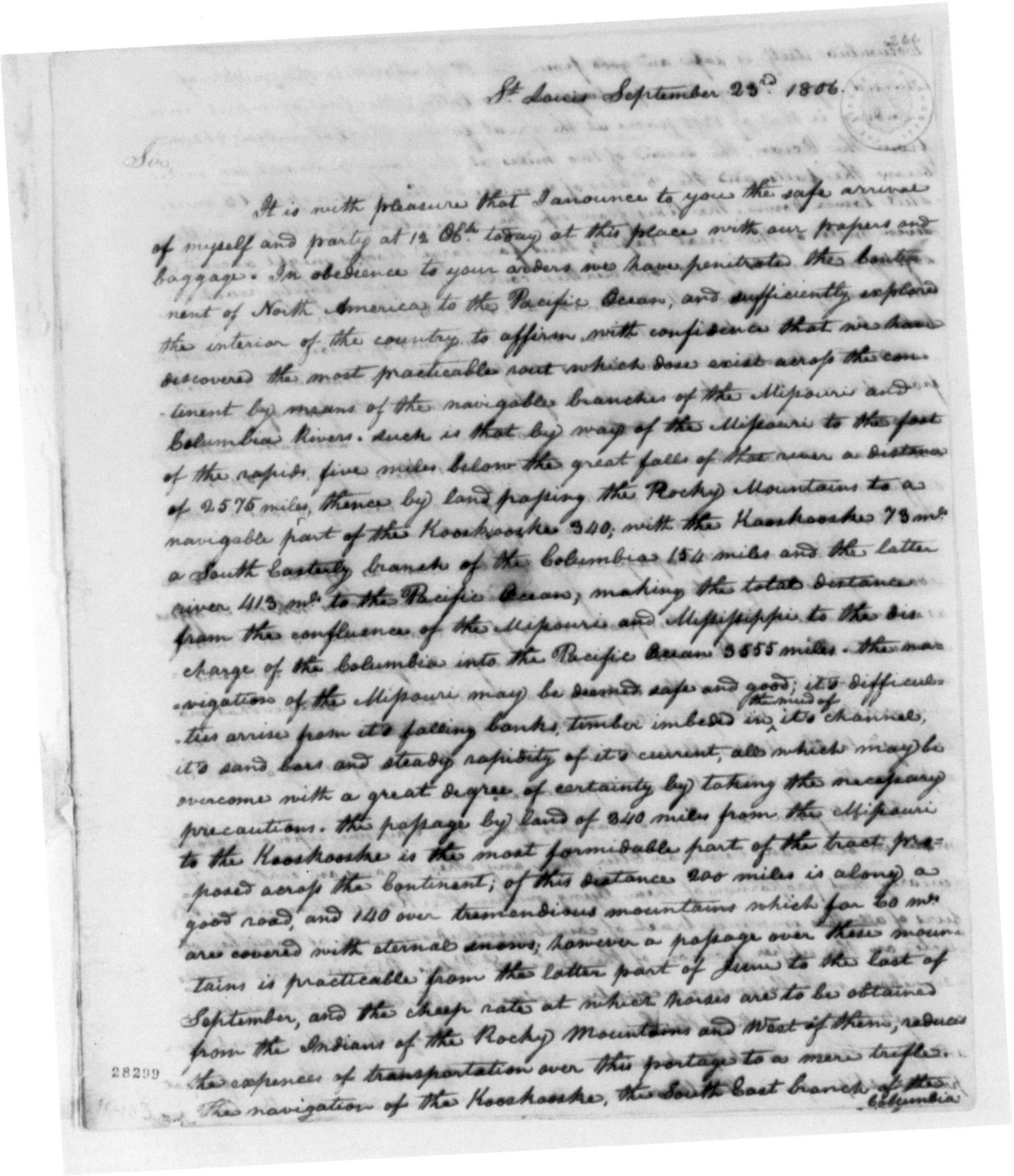

St. Louis September 23rd 1806.

Sir,

It is with pleasure that I anounce to you the safe arrival of myself and party at 12 Oclk. today at this place with our papers and baggage. In obedience to your orders we have penitrated the Continent of North America to the Pacific Ocean, and sufficiently explored the interior of the country to affirm with confidence that we have discovered the most practicable rout which dose exist across the continent by means of the navigable branches of the Missouri and Columbia Rivers. such is that by way of the Missouri to the foot of the rapids five miles below the great falls of that river a distance of 2575 miles, thence by land passing the Rocky Mountains to a navigable part of the Kooskooske 340, with the Kooskooske 73 mls. a South Easterly branch of the Columbia 154 miles and the latter river 413 mls. to the Pacific Ocean; making the total distance from the confluence of the Missouri and Mississippi to the discharge of the Columbia into the Pacific Ocean 3555 miles. the navigation of the Missouri may be deemed safe and good; it's difficulties arrise from it's falling banks, timber imbeded in the mud of it's channel, it's sand bars and steady rapidity of it's current, all which may be overcome with a great degree of certainty by taking the necessary precautions. the passage by land of 340 miles from the Missouri to the Kooskooske is the most formidable part of the tract proposed across the Continent; of this distance 200 miles is along a good road, and 140 over tremendious mountains which for 60 mls. are covered with eternal snows; however a passage over these mountains is practicable from the latter part of June to the last of September, and the cheap rate at which horses are to be obtained from the Indians of the Rocky Mountains and West of them, reduces the expences of transportation over this portage to a mere trifle. The navigation of the Kooskooske, the South East branch of the Columbia

28299

Within hours of having completed the mission assigned to him by Jefferson, Meriwether Lewis sat down on September 23, 1806, to pen his report to Thomas Jefferson. *Library of Congress*

The reports the captains had sent back from Fort Mandan in April 1805 had already been published and circulated, although the captains had no way of knowing this before their return, 17 months later. Although the conventional wisdom was that Lewis and Clark would never return, the appetites of a new generation of explorers had already been whetted.

Neither of them knew that Jefferson was still president, although they seem to have assumed that he would win the 1804 election. He had beat Charles Pinkney 162 to 14 in the Electoral College. Aaron Burr, Jefferson's temperamental vice president at the time that Lewis and Clark started out, had created a bit of a stir when he gunned down former Treasury Secretary Alexander Hamilton in a duel in July 1804. Burr was not renominated. George Clinton was now vice president.

Lewis reached Washington, D.C., in person on December 28 and was delayed throughout his journey by prominent people who wished to wine and dine the great explorer. He reported to Jefferson personally and introduced Chief Sheheke to the president. Lewis spent the better part of three months at the White House going over his journals with Jefferson, and Congress voted a special compensation package for members of the Corps of Discovery that included generous land grants.

In March 1807, Congress confirmed Lewis as the new governor of the Louisiana Territory, which at that time included all of the Louisiana Purchase except the present state of Louisiana, which was then the Territory of Orleans. Clark was named superintendent of Indian Affairs for Louisiana and given the rank of brigadier general.

Both Lewis and Clark were involved in the herculean effort of preparing the journals for publication, but it would not happen in Lewis' lifetime. The first published edition of journals from the expedition was neither those of Lewis nor Clark, but those of Patrick Gass. His were published in 1807, just a year after the expedition returned.

If the success in getting the Lewis and Clark journals back to the "U' States" intact had represented phenomenal luck, the failure to get them into print represented long delays and proportional bad luck. Finally, the edition edited by Nicholas Biddle was published in 1814. It was an enormous volume, but he had left out a great deal of the biological observations. The complete journals, edited by Reuben Thwaites, were finally published in eight volumes in 1904. The definitive version in print today was edited by Gary Moulton and published by the University of Nebraska Press. Its 13 volumes contain the complete journals of Lewis and Clark and the other members of the Corps who kept journals.

Meriwether Lewis did not live to see the journals published. He died on the morning of October 11, 1809, in what is now Lewis County, Tennessee, while en route from St. Louis to Washington to work on the journal project. The cause of death was officially suicide. Lewis had become deeply depressed during his final years and had exhibited suicidal tendencies, possibly exacerbated by troubles in his job as governor, a failed love affair, alcoholism,

Washington Oct. 20. 06

I recieved, my dear Sir, with unspeakable joy your letter of Sep. 23. announcing the return of yourself, Capt Clarke & your party in good health to St. Louis. the unknown scenes in which you were engaged & the length of time without hearing of you had begun to be felt awfully. your letter having been 31. days coming, this cannot find you at Louisville, & I therefore think it safest to lodge it at Charlottesville. it's only object is to assure you of what you already know, my constant affection for you & the joy with which all your friends here will recieve you. tell my friend of Mandane also that I have already opened my arms to recieve him. perhaps, while in our neighborhood, it may be gratifying to him, & accomodation to yourself to take a ride to Monticello and see in what manner I have arranged the tokens of friendship I have recieved from his country particularly as well as from other Indian friends: that I am in fact preparing a kind of Indian hall. mr Dinsmore, my principal workman will shew you every thing there. had you not better bring him by Richmond, Fredericksburg, & Alexandria? he will thus see what none of the others have visited & the convenience of the public stages will facilitate your taking that route. I salute you with sincere affection.

Th: Jefferson

Capt M. Lewis

After he received the September 23 report from Lewis, Thomas Jefferson dashed off this reply on October 20, 1806. *Library of Congress*

frustration over the journals, and/or his consumption of Rush's Pills. Through the years, conspiracy theories have also suggested that he may have been murdered.

William Clark lived a long and successful life. As superintendent of Indian Affairs, he negotiated treaties and constructed frontier outposts. He served as governor of Missouri Territory from 1813 to 1821 and returned to his Indian Affairs job, which he served until his death in 1838. He married Julia Hancock in 1808, and they named their son Meriwether Lewis Clark. The elder Clark freed his slave, York, sometime after 1811, and York went into the freight hauling business.

Most of the members of the expedition eventually settled in Kentucky or farther west. Some remained in the U.S. Army for a time, and several returned to the interior of the continent they had "discovered." The later lives of some of the men are unknown, but there is good information about the sergeants. John Pryor headed the first official sequel to the Lewis and Clark expedition, the 1807 effort to return Mandan Chief Sheheke to his home on the Knife River. This expedition failed when they were attacked by the Sioux and Arikara. Sheheke would not return home until 1809. Pryor married an Osage woman and lived with the tribe until his death in 1831. John Ordway eventually became a prosperous citizen of Missouri and died there in

This season pass admitted L. N. Schlesinger to the 1,240-acre fairgrounds at the Louisiana Purchase Exposition. The fair was such a big deal that the 1904 Olympics were held in St. Louis during the fair, instead of in Chicago, as had been planned. *Library of Congress*

1817. Patrick Gass published his journals, served in the Army through the War of 1812, settled in West Virginia, and died in 1870. He was the last survivor of the Corps of Discovery.

Of the others, John Boley returned from Fort Mandan in 1805 and joined Zebulon Pike on his expeditions into the interior in 1805 and 1806, while Lewis and Clark were still on the trail. George Shannon, the youngest member of the Corps, returned north with Pryor's expedition in 1807, lost a leg in the fight with the Sioux, but later prospered. He became an attorney and later served as a senator from Missouri. He died in 1836.

John Colter was the most famous of the Corps members to go back into the wilderness and became a legendary mountain man. He received his discharge at Fort Mandan in 1806 and led an expedition back up the Missouri River. He spent most of his remaining years as a trapper in or near Montana. He and Corps veteran John Potts were captured by the Blackfeet near Three Forks in 1808. Potts was killed, and Colter's escape became one of the enduring legends of the Old West. Colter finally reached Missouri in 1810 and died three years later. He is best remembered for discovering what became Yellowstone Park and for telling fantastic—albeit true—tales about the place that nobody believed.

George Drouillard, arguably the best woodsman in the Corps, also returned to Montana as a trapper, but he was killed by the Blackfeet near Three Forks in 1810.

Sacagawea, the Shoshone teenager who had such an impact on the expedition and its legacy, remained at Knife River with Toussaint Charbonneau until 1809, when they traveled to St. Louis with their four-year-old son, Jean Baptiste. The boy remained with Clark to be educated under his supervision, and Sacagawea and Charbonneau returned to Knife River. She is believed to have died in December 1812 at the time of, or as a result of complications

The centennial of the Lewis and Clark expedition was celebrated with World's Fairs at both ends of the route. In St. Louis, it took place in Forest Park and was called the Louisiana Purchase Exposition. This panorama was taken from the top of the Festival Hall. *Library of Congress*

Dear Adele, - I just came back from a ride in an auto and enjoyed it very much. Love Charles.

OFFICIAL MAILING CARD
LEWIS & CLARK CENTENNIAL, 1905
PORTLAND, OREGON.

FORESTRY BUILDING. PRINTED IN GERMANY. PUBLISHED BY B.B. RICH, OFFICIAL STATIONER.

In 1905, Portland, Oregon, celebrated with the Lewis and Clark Centennial Exposition, which was designed to acknowledge the captains and promote Portland and Oregon. The 20,600-square-foot Forestry Building heralded the Oregon lumber industry.

Author collection

AGRICULTURAL PALACE

PUBLISHED BY E.P. CHARLTON & CO. PORTLAND, OR.

LEWIS & CLARK EXPOSITION

Your Bro. W. M. Smith.

Oregon's Willamette Valley, the lush terminus of the Oregon Trail in the nineteenth century, produced abundant crops that were acclaimed in 1905 at the 96,600-square-foot Agricultural Palace at the Lewis and Clark Centennial Exposition.

Author collection

pertaining to, the birth of her second child, Lisette. Having been placed on Clark's official Indian Affairs payroll as an interpreter and guide, Charbonneau remained at Knife River until his death around 1843.

Young Jean Baptiste was educated in St. Louis but followed in his father's footsteps as a wilderness guide. After performing in this role on behalf of Prince Paul of Wurtemberg, he was invited to Germany, where he remained for six years. He returned to the West, where he worked as a guide. He traveled to California, where he served as alcalde, or mayor, of

Scott Mandrell, as Meriwether Lewis, poses with his horse prior to departing Harpers Ferry for Pittsburgh on July 8, 2003. Mandrell, a school teacher from Alton, Illinois, is a member of the Discovery Expedition of St. Charles, Missouri. Members of this group are the official re-enactors of the national 2003–2006 Lewis and Clark bicentennial commemoration. *NPS photo by David T. Gilbert*

Mission San Luis Rey, near Oceanside, after it was appropriated from the Church by Pio Pico in 1845. Jean Baptiste joined the California Gold Rush in 1848 and remained in the Sierra Nevada for many years and managed a hotel in Auburn. He died in Oregon in 1866, while on the trail to another Gold Rush in Montana.

Jean Baptiste is now a mere historic footnote, but his mother remains one of the most enduring characters from the Expedition. Numerous reminders of her have been produced through the years, from postage stamps to the dollar coin with her likeness that was issued by the U.S. Mint in 2000. Although she almost certainly died in her twenties, legends continued to persist that she was still alive. A widely publicized rumor circulated in the early twentieth century, stating that a woman who had died on the Wind River Reservation in Wyoming in 1884 was Sacagawea.

Whatever the case, Sacagawea, as well as the captains who benefited from her services, have achieved immortality. Their names and their memories will continue to live on and cast a wide shadow across that broad arc of the American interior where they once traveled.

Designed by Glenna Goodacre of Santa Fe, New Mexico, the Sacagawea dollar was first issued by the United States Mint in 2000. *Author collection*

This is the bust of William Clark at his gravesite at Bellefontaine Cemetery in St. Louis. He outlived Meriwether Lewis by nearly three decades but spent those decades near where he and Lewis began and ended their adventure. *Missouri Tourism New Bureau*

The cleft in the cliffs in the background is the upstream portal of what Meriwether Lewis happily designated as the "Gates of the Rocky Mountains." In fact, he was still many weeks from actually entering the mountains. *Bill Yenne*

Index

Lewis and Clark Lager was created as a bicentennial celebration by the Lewis and Clark Brewery, located in Helena, Montana, the seat of the only county in the United States named for Lewis and Clark. The company was originally known as the Sleeping Giant Brewery, named for the predominant mountain in the Big Belt Range north of Helena. *Courtesy of the Lewis and Clark Brewery*